Washington Historic Landmarks.

Pillars of Patriotism

MOLLIE SOMERVILLE

National Society Daughters of the American Revolution, Washington, D.C. • 1890-1986

OFFICIAL DAR INSIGNIA

"The official insignia of the National Society shall be in the form of a spinning wheel and distaff. The wheel shall be seven-eighths of an inch in diameter and of gold, with thirteen spokes and a field of dark blue enamel upon the rim bearing the name DAUGHTERS OF THE AMERICAN REVOLUTION in letters of gold; upon the outer edge of the wheel, opposite the ends of the wheel, opposite the ends of the spokes, are thirteen small stars which may be set with precious stones at the discretion of the owner; underneath the wheel a golden distaff, one-and-one-half inches long, filled with platinum or white gold flax. . . ."

OFFICIAL DAR SEAL

"The Seal of the National Society shall be charged with the figure of a Dame of the period of the American Revolution sitting at her spinning wheel, with thirteen stars above her, the whole surrounded by a rim containing the name, 'The National Society of the Daughters of the American Revolution', the motto, 'God, Home and Country', and the dates '1776' and '1890'."

Copyright © 1985 by The National Society, Daughters of the American Revolution
Published by The National Society, Daughters of the American Revolution
Library of Congress Catalogue Card Number 84-60114
ISBN 0-9602528-7-8

Design by Leckie/Lehmann, Washington, DC
Photographs by Arthur Vitols, unless otherwise credited.
Typesetting by Hodges Typographers, Silver Spring, MD
Printing by Garamond/Pridemark Press, Baltimore, MD

Front cover: Memorial Continental Hall
Back cover: Constitution Hall
Cover photographs by Robert C. Lautman, Washington, DC

Foreword

"God, Home and Country" is the motto of the Daughters of the American Revolution. These words inspire Daughters to dedicate themselves to the historical, educational and patriotic objectives of the National Society and serve as a reminder of the loyalty we as citizens of this great Nation pledge to our Country.

This book, an update of two previous publications, is an effort to present to members and the general public the story of the National Society, Daughters of the American Revolution, and its service to mankind. May it serve to encourage patriotism and service for all who read it, and especially for those whose efforts and dedication have made possible the continuation of progress reflected by the buildings in the City of Washington, which are known as the National Headquarters of the Daughters of the American Revolution. Within one city block, enhancing the beauty of the Ellipse, Memorial Continental Hall and Constitution Hall, connected by the Administration Building, house a genealogy library, period rooms, a museum, an Americana collection of documents and an historical research library. These treasures the Daughters generously share with all who are interested in the preservation of our great heritage.

In 1985, the Continental Congress overwhelmingly adopted as an ongoing project of the current and future administrations the climate control of Memorial Continental Hall and the Administration Building. Consistent temperature and humidity control will preserve the priceless collections in these buildings. The construction in Memorial Continental Hall will conform to the code established by the National Park Service for an historic landmark and the integrity of both buildings will be maintained.

Memorial Continental Hall and Constitution Hall have been designated as National Historic Landmarks. We can be proud of these distinctions, but take our greatest pride in the service represented by the National Headquarters buildings.

As we turn the pages of this book and share the memories of our past accomplishments, may we accept the challenge of the future of the Society.

Sarah M. King

Mrs. Walter Hughey King
President General, NSDAR

Acknowledgements

This is my third book on the story of the National Society of the Daughters of the American Revolution. I began the research for the first of these books in 1962: "In Washington" appeared in 1965. Eleven years later "Washington Landmark" was published. The many changes that have occurred since then necessitate a newly revised and up-dated publication: "Washington Historic Landmarks" is the result.

The photographs in all three books have been by Arthur Vitols, except where indicated otherwise.

The writing and compilation of "Washington Historic Landmarks" and the two earlier books were made possible by the help of numerous people at the National Headquarters of the Daughters. But most of the 1962 staff members are gone, and there have been many staff changes between 1962 and 1986. So, in expressing my gratitude, I will list those offices alphabetically whose members have assisted me over the years.

I thank the staff of the Archives, Corresponding Secretary General, Curator General, DAR Magazine, Historian General, Librarian General, Organizing Secretary General, President General, Recording Secretary General, Registrar General, and Treasurer General for their invaluable help, rendered so graciously and understandingly.

My special thanks are to the Presidents General who authorized the books: the late Mrs. Robert V. H. Duncan, Mrs. Wakelee Rawson Smith, and Mrs. Walter Hughey King, respectively.

Mrs. Eldred Martin Yochim, First Vice President General, has aided my endeavors ever since I began writing for the DAR. Thank you, Marie, for your support these twenty-three years.

And, finally, I thank Mrs. R. Hugh Reid, National Parliamentarian, whose patience and competence as advisor enabled me to meet the publication deadline date of this book.

M.S.

Contents

5   Foreword

6   Acknowledgments

9   Washington City, circa 1890

13   **PART I   A GUIDE TO THE NATIONAL HEADQUARTERS**

15   **Memorial Continental Hall**

23   The Library

26   The State Period Rooms

49   **Administration Building**

51   The Museum

56   The Presidents General

58   The Atrium

59   The Presidents General Assembly Room

60   The Americana Collection,
The Special Collection Pertaining to NSDAR History,
and the NSDAR Archives

63   Seimes Microfilm Center

63   Historical Research Library

65   **Constitution Hall**

71   **PART II   THE STORY OF THE DAUGHTERS**

73   **The Founders**

75   **Historical, Educational, and Patriotic Pursuits**

90   **An Overview, 1890 & 1986**

94   **Major National and International Gifts or Commemorations**

First Continental Congress, February 22, 1892, held at the Church of Our Father, 13th & L Streets, N.W., Washington, D. C.

Washington City, circa 1890

The years between the centennial celebration of our birth as a Nation and the approaching 400th anniversary of the discovery of the New World (1876-1892) were marked by a revival in patriotism and an intense interest in the beginnings of the United States of America. Men were offered opportunities to perpetuate the memory of ancestors who fought to make this country free and independent by joining associations such as the Society of the Cincinnati, which dates from the close of the American Revolution, the Sons of Revolutionary Sires, the Sons of the Revolution, and the Sons of the American Revolution. But women, too, felt the desire to express their patriotic feelings and were frustrated at the lack of opportunities by which they could do so. Among them were several in the Nation's capital who decided to organize under the name Daughters of the American Revolution.

During the summer of 1890 these women performed preliminary organizational work and invited Mrs. Benjamin Harrison, the wife of the President of the United States, to be their President General.

A meeting for the organization of the National Society of the Daughters of the American Revolution was . . . held at the Strathmore Arms, 810 12th Street, Washington, D.C., at half past two o'clock in the afternoon of Saturday, October 11, 1890.

The meeting of October 11th recessed until the afternoon of October 18th, when the letter of acceptance from Mrs. Harrison was read. Caroline Scott Harrison was unanimously elected first President General.

Then a motion was adopted for erecting a fireproof memorial building, to provide a place for historical relics and to serve as a home for the Society.

Thus, in one afternoon, the Society was well on the way toward national recognition: it had chosen a nationally-known woman as President General and had resolved to build a national headquarters building in the Nation's capital.

When newspapers across the country in mid-October 1890 spread word of the formation of a new society of women calling themselves

The first home of the Daughters of the American Revolution: the residence of Prof. and Mrs. William D. Cabell at 1407-1409 Massachusetts Avenue, Washington City. Here the Board of Management met monthly during the Society's early years.

Daughters of the American Revolution, headed by Mrs. Benjamin Harrison, the First Lady, national interest was aroused. But "there was in some quarters great doubt as to the success of the movement. Letters came from both East and West asking 'what was it for,' and what practical good we expected to accomplish. The question of 'social equality' disturbed some; others, opposed to women being in public work, feared it would 'demoralize all who had escaped the suffrage fever.' Society in Washington was watching critically before committing itself."

It soon became evident to the Vice President General Presiding, Mrs. William D. Cabell, and the Board of Management that something must be done quickly to answer these questions and to make it clear that the organization was based upon American ideas of patriotism. It was decided that this something which would give the Society the necessary social prestige associated with the City of Washington would be a grand reception attended by the First Lady.

On February 22, 1891, when the Society was only a few months old, the "grand reception" honoring the Daughters of the American Revolution was held at the home of Professor and Mrs. Cabell, 1407-1409 Massachusetts Avenue. Before moving to Washington, Professor Cabell had conducted a school for boys in Norwood, Virginia. In Washington, Mrs. Cabell opened a school for young girls in their home and named it Norwood Institute. Its double drawing room provided ideal space for a large gathering. The Sons of the American Revolution were invited.

In spite of a sleet storm, several hundred ladies and gentlemen attended the reception, wearing the blue and white rosettes of the two Societies. Red, white, and blue bunting draped every door and was looped from window to window. Members of the Washington Continental Guards, in their buff and blue uniforms, formed a double line in the hall. Mrs. Harrison, in a black moire silk and old rose satin dress, with jet trimmings, received with the hostess, Mrs. Cabell, who was dressed in dark velvet with lighter silk and steel trimmings. Entertainment was provided by solo artists assisted by a chorus of Norwood Institute students. Eight of the young ladies, dressed in colonial costume, danced a minuet with the uniformed guardsmen as partners.

In the supper rooms the colors of the Society were reproduced in flowers and decorations, and everything was done to arouse pride in heroic, national ancestry, that alone gave the right of entrance to the new organization.

The story of this reception in Washington, marked by the spirit of patriotism in speech and song, reached to the far ends of the country, and success was assured. Newspapers took up the cry and sent the intelligence over the land. Application papers began to pour in. The American women were awakened by this revelation, and now "What is it for?" was answered—"It is not for an aristocracy but to honor the men who carried the muskets, and the boys who beat the drums and fifed 'Yankee Doodle' for liberty; to honor the women who served the country in their homes, while the men were away fighting battles for freedom; and that their names should be rescued from the musty annals of the Revolution, and for the first time inscribed on the pages of history, as factors in making the Nation. Both these men and women were at last having their names placed on the 'Roll of Honor' beside those of the officers and leaders in the American Revolution. . . ."

The Society celebrated its first anniversary with a membership of 818, the Charter Members. In December, 1891, it was resolved to set aside specified funds for a national headquarters building.

Before the First Continental Congress adjourned, an invitation was received from the famous photographer, Mathew B. Brady, asking "the privilege of making a photographic group of the Society, to be added to my historical collection of the most eminent people of the world."

In the front row: Mrs. Benjamin Harrison, center, Mrs. William D. Cabell on her right, Miss Eugenia Washington and Miss Mary Desha on her left; in the second row: Mrs. Ellen Hardin Walworth and Miss Mary S. Lockwood between Mrs. Harrison and Miss Washington.

*The National Society of Daughters of the American
Revolution was organized in the parlors of the home of
Mary S. Lockwood (a Founder), 810 12th Street, Washington
City on October 11, 1890 at two o'clock in the afternoon.*
Washingtoniana Division, D.C. Public Library.

*Looking west along F Street where NSDAR rented offices in two different
buildings between 1893 and 1910.* Washingtoniana Division, D.C. Public Library.

*The Continental Congresses of 1898
through 1904 were held in the Grand
Opera House, 1424 Pennsylvania
Avenue, Washington City.*
Washingtoniana Division, D.C. Public Library.

PART I

A Guide to the National Headquarters

15 MEMORIAL CONTINENTAL HALL

23 The Library
26 The State Period Rooms

49 ADMINISTRATION BUILDING

51 The Museum
56 The Presidents General
58 The Atrium
59 The Assembly Room
60 The Americana Collection
63 Seimes Microfilm Center
63 Historical Research Library

65 CONSTITUTION HALL

Thirteen monolithic columns support the roof of the Memorial Portico on the south side of Memorial Continental Hall. These columns were presented by chapters or legislatures of the thirteen original States and are named for these States. Many diplomatic and official government functions were held in Memorial Continental Hall auditorium and the Memorial Portico entrance was used by the President of the United States when he attended them. A 1790 map of the capital city indicated that squares were to be divided among the States on which they would erect "Statues, Columns, Obelisks. . . ." This plan was not followed. The Memorial Portico at National Headquarters of the Daughters of the American Revolution in the Nation's capital represents that architectural tribute to the thirteen original States.

Memorial Continental Hall

The National Headquarters of the Daughters of the American Revolution is in Washington, D.C., on Seventeenth Street, between the
Washington Monument and the White House, opposite the President's Park, now known as the Ellipse. Memorial Continental Hall,
the Society's white marble headquarters building, faces the Ellipse
and it is the first of the three-structures-in-one built by the Daughters
which encompass an entire city block. This group of buildings is the
largest and most beautiful of its kind in the world that is owned and
maintained exclusively by women.

When the Daughters purchased the site for Memorial Continental
Hall in 1902 they were called "foolhardy women" by the newspapers
of the day. It was known that there were underground springs in one
corner of the property. As for the location, they were advised that the
area would remain largely undeveloped for the foreseeable future.
But the Daughters, who at first had hoped that the United States
Congress would give them a piece of ground (and, in fact, a site was
given them but a clause in the title prevented erecting a building on it),
were determined to go ahead with their plans. They correctly pre-
dicted that the section of the Capital City south of F Street and west of
Seventeenth Street would develop favorably for them and that it
would do so sooner than expected. Pierre L'Enfant's *Plan for the City
of Washington* of 1792, which had been supervised and approved by
George Washington, supported their hopes even though more than a
hundred years later the plot plan of their newly-bought site showed it
as opposite the White Lot, so-named because a white picket fence
enclosed the grazing grounds of the presidential cattle.

The Daughters' lot extended from C to D Streets on Seventeenth
Street, a distance of 200 feet, and a little less than half that length along
both C and D Streets.

A block to the north of the building site was the Corcoran Gallery of
Art. To the south was Van Ness Park, where the farm cottage of David
Burnes had stood a hundred years before (and where the Pan American Union Building stands today). Burnes was an original landowner
whose farm, extending beyond Pennsylvania Avenue, had included
the National Society headquarters building site. When the Federal
City was being laid out, farmer Burnes stubbornly defied President

George Washington, whose road engineers stood ready to cut a swath representing Pennsylvania Avenue through the ripening fields. Road building operations were delayed until Burnes harvested his crop.

In 1818, the Mayor of Washington, Captain Thomas Carbery, had built his house, a substantial brick structure, on the same lot the Daughters later bought.

By the purchase of the site for Memorial Continental Hall, the Society took the first step toward realizing the dream of a "house beautiful" envisioned since its founding twelve years before. The early records repeatedly allude to this: the phrase "a fireproof building" occurs again and again. At the second organizational meeting on October 18, 1890, a resolution was adopted ". . . to provide a place for the collection of Historical relics. . . . This may first be in rooms, and later in the erection of a fireproof building." In 1892, at the First Continental Congress (the Society's annual meeting), the amount of $650 was reported as having been set aside for this purpose. In December of that year, $75 was contributed from the proceeds of a tea held at Monticello, Thomas Jefferson's home.

On October 11, 1902, ground was broken for Memorial Continental Hall and the site marked with a piece of granite which came from one of the original window sills of the White House. A flag pole was erected and a Flag presented by the Sons of the American Revolution floated over the site. The cornerstone was laid with Masonic ceremonies on April 19, 1904, the gavel being the same one that George Washington had used in laying the cornerstone of the United States Capitol in 1793.

The April 19th date is significant. At the Twelfth Continental Congress in 1903, the date of the annual meeting was changed from February 22nd (Washington's birthday) to April 19th (anniversary of the Battle of Lexington). The change was made to assure better weather conditions, but a Louisiana Daughter favored the new date because the February one conflicted with Mardi Gras.

The Continental Congress of 1905 was the first one to be held in Memorial Continental Hall, still only partially completed. Birds found openings in the temporary canvas roof stretched across the auditorium seating 1,666 and their excited twittering formed a musical background to the business sessions below.

When Memorial Continental Hall was completed, *The Washington Evening Star* reported: "This Valhalla is unique. It is the costliest and most impressive monument of its kind ever built by women in this country or any other. Many other halls of fame have been erected and other grand monuments consecrated to the memory of some individual heroic figure in the history of our nation, but this is the first building dedicated to all the recognized heroes of the American Revolution: men and women alike. From the artistic standpoint it is one of the finest buildings which the beautiful Capital contains, and from the utilitarian it is destined to become one of the most useful."

The officers and clerical staff of the Society were eager to move into the spacious marble headquarters building. In the very early days, the officers kept their records at home. Late in December, 1891, they authorized renting an office, "paying for the same $20.00 a month," purchasing the necessary furniture, including a safe, and installing a clerk to be paid $25 a month.

A room was rented at 1505 Pennsylvania Avenue. It was "a little room in an upper story . . . scarcely large enough to comfortably seat the members of the Board." But it was diagonally across the street from the White House and very convenient for Mrs. Harrison to preside at the monthly meetings.

The clerk was Miss Mary Ball, the first of three sisters who successively served the Society in this capacity. At a meeting the summer of 1892, the Board resolved to "give to Miss Ball the month of August as a vacation, her salary to be paid as usual, and that her sister be employed by the Society as a clerk during her absence from the office; provided that Miss Ball assume the entire responsibility of the office, and direct her sister during the month she is employed, seeing that the work necessary is done properly; that the application papers are protected, the magazine for the month of August sent to subscribers, all letters answered, and whatever is necessary and usual, provided for. Otherwise the proposition pertaining to Miss Ball's vacation, and the employing of her sister, is null and void."

After Mrs. Harrison's death, two rooms were leased downtown, in the Kellogg Building, at 1416 F Street, N.W., for one year, from August 1893 to August 1894. The third, and the last office of the Society before moving to Memorial Continental Hall, was six rooms on the third floor of the Washington Loan and Trust Building at 902 F Street, N.W. This building was chosen because it was "fire proof."

When the offices were moved to Memorial Continental Hall early in 1910, the staff, who were accustomed to lunch-hour browsing in the heart of the city's shopping area, missed the downtown department stores. And it was dark before their day's work ended. So the clerks would meet at the bronze doors in the lobby of the Hall and leave the building in a group. Thus reassured as to their safety, they walked in "the wilds" of Seventeenth Street a few blocks north to Pennsylvania Avenue to board the trolleys that would take them home.

A short time after the Society built Memorial Continental Hall, the Pan American Union and the American Red Cross became its immediate neighbors. The United States Government soon followed. Such buildings as the Federal Reserve, the United States Public Health, the Department of the Interior, the National Academy of Sciences, pointing as they do toward the magnificent Lincoln Memorial, have developed that part of Washington into an area possibly unequalled in beauty in any capital in the world.

The Pennsylvania Foyer in Memorial Continental Hall once served as the entrance hall to the National Society's main auditorium, a room which now houses the extensive Genealogical Library. The elaborate architectural detailing reflects the Beaux-Arts training of the building's architect, Edward Pearce Casey (1864-1940). Ten bust portraits of famous Americans by George Attilio and Furio Piccirilli were sculpted around 1910 to encircle this entrance foyer.

Memorial Continental Hall. The plaque is in the entrance corridor.

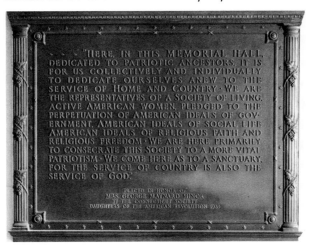

IN RESPONSE
TO AN INVITATION BY THE
PRESIDENT OF THE UNITED STATES
DELEGATES FROM
THE UNITED STATES OF AMERICA • THE BRITISH EMPIRE • FRANCE • ITALY • JAPAN
ASSEMBLED IN THIS AUDITORIUM NOVEMBER 12, 1921
FOR A
CONFERENCE ON THE LIMITATION OF ARMAMENT
TOGETHER WITH DELEGATES FROM
BELGIUM • CHINA • THE NETHERLANDS AND PORTUGAL
INVITED TO PARTICIPATE IN THE DISCUSSION OF
PACIFIC AND FAR EASTERN QUESTIONS

ON FEBRUARY 6, 1922 AT THE CLOSE OF THE
CONFERENCE THE FOLLOWING TREATIES WERE SIGNED BY
REPRESENTATIVES OF THE PARTICIPATING NATIONS

| TREATY LIMITING NAVAL ARMAMENT | TREATY RELATING TO SUBMARINES AND GASES | TREATY RELATING TO INSULAR POSSESSIONS AND INSULAR DOMINIONS IN THE REGION OF THE PACIFIC OCEAN | TREATY RELATING TO POLICIES CONCERNING CHINA | TREATY RELATING TO CHINESE CUSTOMS TARIFF |

THIS TABLET WAS PRESENTED BY THE GOVERNMENT OF THE UNITED STATES
NOV. 12, 1922 AS A TOKEN OF APPRECIATION TO THE OFFICERS OF THE NATIONAL
SOCIETY OF THE DAUGHTERS OF THE AMERICAN REVOLUTION FOR MAKING AVAILABLE
MEMORIAL CONTINENTAL HALL FOR THE SESSIONS OF THE CONFERENCE

CHARLES E. HUGHES
SECRETARY OF STATE
WASHINGTON NOVEMBER 12, 1922

WARREN G. HARDING
PRESIDENT
OF THE UNITED STATES

The Conference on Limitation of Armament was held in Memorial Continental Hall auditorium (now the Library) in 1921-22. The tablet of appreciation presented to the NSDAR by the United States government to mark this historic occasion is mounted on the wall of this room. This was the first time that major powers had consented to disarm.

The plaque outside the 17th Street entrance to Memorial Continental Hall also commemorates the event.

MEMORIAL CONTINENTAL HALL
HAS BEEN DESIGNATED A
REGISTERED NATIONAL
HISTORIC LANDMARK
UNDER THE PROVISIONS OF THE
HISTORIC SITES ACT OF AUGUST 21, 1935
THIS SITE POSSESSES EXCEPTIONAL VALUE
IN COMMEMORATING OR ILLUSTRATING
THE HISTORY OF THE UNITED STATES

U. S. DEPARTMENT OF THE INTERIOR
NATIONAL PARK SERVICE

1973

In Memorial Continental Hall, on either side of the Library entrance, are two magnificent marble stairways extending from the lower level to the third floor, with custom-designed banisters below mahogany rails.

The 26 glass finials atop the newel posts along the two marble stairwells in Memorial Continental Hall symbolize hospitality.

The earliest known photograph of the Museum, circa 1915.

The Banquet Hall on the third floor of Memorial Continental Hall.

In converting Memorial Continental Hall auditorium into the Genealogical Library, the architectural features of this outstandingly beautiful room were preserved, and even the two tiers of boxes were left undisturbed. Twenty-five opaque glass skylights, each nearly eight feet square, bring daylight to the readers' desks sixty feet below. Suspended from the cove-lit cornice around the four walls are the State flags, some of which were designed by Daughters or were the result of contests that Daughters initiated and then were officially adopted by the State legislatures.

The Library

The genealogical resources in the DAR Library make it one of the largest of its kind in the United States. There are special indices to state and local histories and Revolutionary War pensions, files containing Bible records and other sources of information once only in private hands, transcriptions of cemetery markers, and unique compilations of county records. In addition, there are typewritten and bound copies of countless unpublished Bible, court, church, and cemetery records which are available in no other library. These were acquired through the painstaking efforts of Daughters who have copied, verified, and indexed the obscure and difficult-to-find records.

The need for establishing a library was brought before the Daughters at their First Continental Congress. Two years later, the importance of having authentic records and books of reference for the library was again stressed. At that time, there were 42 books valued at about $150 in the Society's collection: $25 was appropriated for purchasing specific publications. Another two years passed before it was deemed necessary to formally establish a library to process the 500-600 applications for membership being received each month. Since its inception in 1896, the DAR Library has grown from 125 books to over 75,000 volumes and 40,000 manuscript files.

Before Memorial Continental Hall was built, the Library's collection was housed in office space rented by the Society. In 1910, the Library moved into the newly completed Memorial Continental Hall, where it occupied the north wing adjacent to the auditorium. The continual growth of the collection warranted allocating a larger space to the Library and in 1930 it was moved to the second floor of Constitution Hall. Since 1949 the Library has occupied its present location in the remodeled auditorium of Memorial Continental Hall. This move was prompted by the necessity to provide more space for the increased number of books. This same pressure caused alterations inside the Library in 1964-1965 when an expansion project removed the remaining balcony seating and created a double-tier area for additional bookshelves and desks.

Although the Library was originally designed as a meeting place for the annual Continental Congress, and a variety of changes had to be

One of the eight-feet-square skylights in the ceiling of the Library and above the two stairways in Memorial Continental Hall.

Rembrandt Peale, son of Charles Wilson Peale, painted George Washington from life in 1795 when the artist was only eighteen years old. From this and other studies he produced a series of portraits of Washington which became known as the "porthole portraits."

made to convert it into a Library, much of the original architecture was retained: only the stage and seats were removed on the main floor. The impressive high arched walls, custom decorated in plaster fruits and leaves, rise past the tiered balconies to the great glass ceiling with ornate ironwork in tracery design. This ceiling permits the entrance of diffused sunlight, high-lighting the architectural design of the Library and enhancing the brilliantly colored State flags.

The original purpose of the Library was to provide authentic documentation to assist the staff genealogists with the approval of membership applications. While this remains a major function, ninety-five years of growth have transformed the Library into a research facility of national importance, and all researchers are welcome. The many rare and unique materials housed in the Library and the visitors from all over the country who use them necessitate the requirement that the collection be strictly for reference use with no loans of materials.

To familiarize potential researchers with the special holdings which they may use in the Library, the DAR has published printed catalogs of the collection. The first such bibliography appeared in 1920 and was expanded and reissued in 1940. The growth of the Library over the next forty years necessitated a major overhaul of the organization of the books and the card catalog. From 1980 to 1985 the Reclassification Project transformed the Library into a better organized and more easily managed collection. Another result of this project was the publication of a new *Library Catalog* in two volumes which serves as a major addition to the national bibliographic literature for genealogy and local history.

Researchers may use the Library Monday through Friday 9:00 a.m. to 4:00 p.m., with the exception of holidays, and on certain Sunday afternoons from 1:00 to 5:00. The facilities are closed to the public during the month of April to accommodate the many members who come to Washington for the Society's Continental Congress.

The State Period Rooms

Almost a century ago, the Daughters set as a priority goal the preservation of "relics" that would accumulate over the years, and they have held steadfastly to that objective. At their organizational meetings it was proposed to build a national headquarters. Later, the DAR state

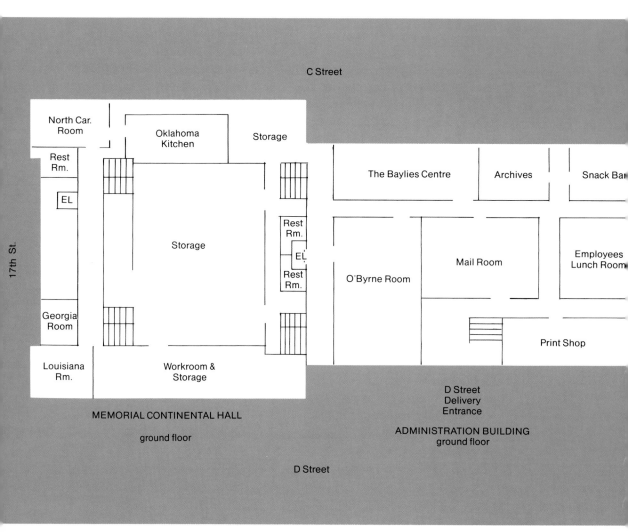

C Street

North Car. Room

Oklahoma Kitchen

Storage

The Baylies Centre

Archives

Snack Bar

Rest Rm.

EL

17th St.

Storage

Rest Rm.

EL

Rest Rm.

O'Byrne Room

Mail Room

Employees Lunch Room

Georgia Room

Louisiana Rm.

Workroom & Storage

Print Shop

MEMORIAL CONTINENTAL HALL

ground floor

D Street
Delivery
Entrance

ADMINISTRATION BUILDING
ground floor

D Street

organizations assisted by paying for specified rooms in the building, and then by providing funds for their furnishings or actually donating some of the furniture. When the staff moved into Memorial Continental Hall on February 28, 1910, the building was partly furnished.

All the state organizations, whether they had a State Room or not, contributed to the construction of the National Headquarters buildings and provided generously for furnishing and equipping them.

Most of the rooms were designated as offices but some were furnished as meeting rooms. The first such meeting room, the New Jersey State Room, which looks very much like it did when it was furnished prior to 1911, expresses the patriotic endeavors of the Society. Through the efforts of New Jersey Daughters, the British frigate *Augusta*, which sank during the Battle of Red Bank on October 23, 1777, was raised and part of the vessel salvaged to carve the paneling and furnishings for the New Jersey State Room. Even those intended as offices, such as the Indiana Period Room which honored the first President General, Mrs. Benjamin Harrison, a native of that

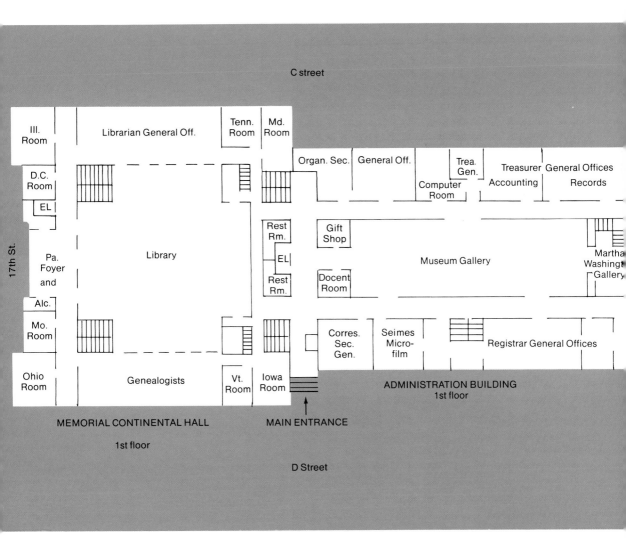

state, was furnished appropriately in keeping with the high position of the occupant. It is of interest that when the Administration Building was constructed during Mrs. George Maynard Minor's term as President General, the Connecticut Daughters honored her similarly.

As the work of the Society increased, more and more rooms were needed by the staff. At the same time, the increased membership donated more and more family heirlooms and historical relics to their State Rooms, giving them the appearance of regional, or period American homes. The available space had to accommodate desks and file cabinets as well as these lovely gifts. At the times when the Continental Congress or the Board of Management met, there was no room for the Daughters of a particular state to meet in their State Room for group discussions. In 1920, it was decided to build a separate building where the work of the Society could be carried on and to devote Memorial Continental Hall to its memorial purposes. Today there are thirty-three rooms at National Headquarters depicting regional and

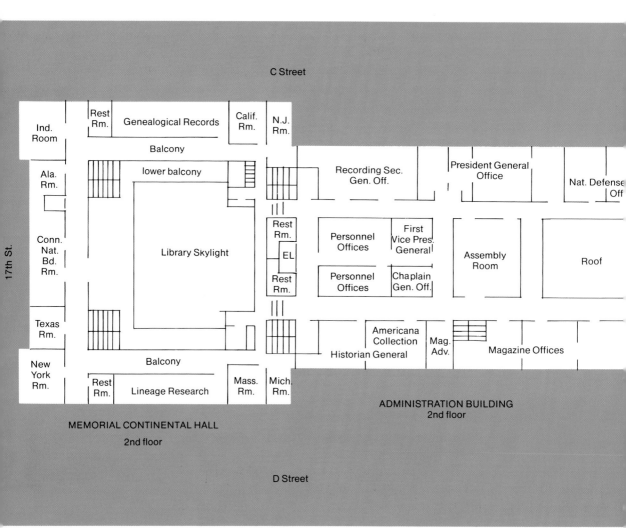

domestic scenes of American life. Most of these have a cut-off date of 1830. States that came into the Union after 1830 may propose objects for their rooms post-dating 1830 for approval of the Office of the Curator General.

In keeping with the general plan that Memorial Continental Hall in its entirety be an outstanding museum, the State Period Rooms have become a focal point of interest to the general public. The DAR motto, "God, Home and Country," is brought to life in the collections of domestic objects displayed. Covering the Colonial, Revolutionary, and Federal periods in American history, the daily life from the seventeenth through the mid-nineteenth centuries are depicted here. Some items of a later date that are of particular interest to the Society, or of national importance, are also included.

There is no connecting passageway between Memorial Continental Hall and the Administration Building on the Third Floor.

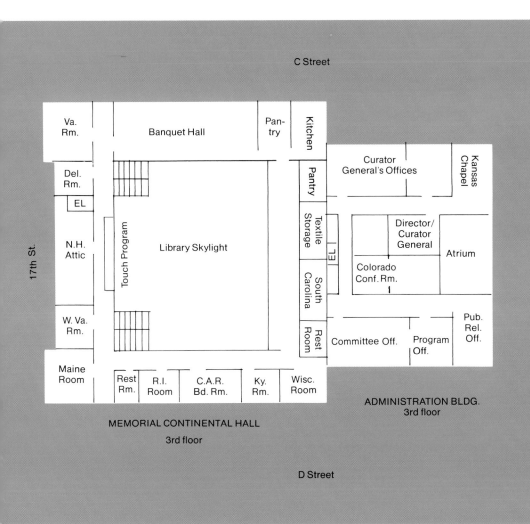

A total of five states have reinstalled or installed period rooms in Memorial Continental Hall since 1976. Re-installations include: the California Room which recreates a whaling station in Monterey; the mid-19th century stencil-decorated Texas Room copied from a home in Alleyton; and, the Louisiana gallery-like installation of locally-made furniture and decorative arts. The states of Georgia and South Carolina have recently installed period rooms. Georgia modeled its interior on the long room in Peter Tondee's Tavern in Savannah, ca. 1775, while the South Carolina Room depicts a bedroom dressed for the summer season.

ALABAMA   The Alabama Room has served many purposes. In 1911 it was designated as a reception room for the President General and during World War II it was used as an office by the American Red Cross. In 1946 it was redecorated as a parlor with furnishings in the Empire style of the 1830s and 40s. Of particular interest is the Gothic Revival secretary bookcase which was originally owned by William Rufus King, Vice President during the administration of President Franklin Pierce.

CALIFORNIA The white-washed walls and exposed ceiling beams of the California Room are suggestive of California adobe architecture of the 1860s. Modeled after a whaling station in Monterey, California, the room is furnished with objects representing the many different cultures which came together in California. Furniture in the Anglo-American style is used with accessories of Oriental and Spanish-Indian origin.

COLORADO The Colorado Room serves as a conference room for the Office of the Curator General. Frequently used by the Museum staff for teaching or research, the room is also available to visiting scholars who wish to examine objects from the Museum's collections. The framed Navaho rug is a reminder of Colorado's native heritage.

CONNECTICUT   The Connecticut Board Room (1904-1906) is the room in which the National Board of Management meets. A reliance on the classical principles of architecture, an emphasis on symmetry, and an elaborate stucco relief decoration highlighted with gilding identify this room as an example of early twentieth-century Beaux-Arts architecture.

DELAWARE   The Delaware Room was installed in 1956. The mid eighteenth-century paneling came from the Goodwin House in Stratford, Connecticut, and the wide-board flooring, hearth bricks, nails and hardware came from an early nineteenth-century home in Ware, Massachusetts. The walnut side chair and the upholstered mahogany side chair are probably of Delaware origin.

DISTRICT OF COLUMBIA The District of Columbia Room is furnished in the Federal style and includes a delicately painted arm chair which was part of a suite of furniture used by Colonel John Tayloe in his Washington townhouse, The Octagon. Hanging above the German piano is a needlework picture which was probably worked by a young lady attending school in Georgetown.

GEORGIA The Georgia Room is based on Peter Tondee's Tavern in Savannah, Georgia. Although the Tondee Tavern no longer stands, the room is furnished as suggested by Peter Tondee's 1775 estate inventory. His furnishings included twelve windsor chairs, a quantity of pewter and creamware, several pieces of china, and a delft punch bowl.

ILLINOIS   In the Illinois Room the spider-leg table is set with Pittsburgh glass and Chinese export porcelain for the serving of light refreshments. Flanking the fireplace are two late eighteenth-century easy chairs, an embroidered English firescreen, and two American candlestands or small tables. In the background a tall case clock combines a case made by a Philadelphia cabinetmaker with works by Benjamin Reeve of Greenwich, New Jersey.

INDIANA   The Indiana Room suggests a library from a home located along the Eastern seaboard during the early Federal period. The library is well furnished with objects of both American and British manufacture. The secretary-bookcase was made in North Carolina in the late eighteenth century and the tall case clock was made in Indiana, with works by Humphrey Griffith of Indianapolis, ca. 1830. The pastel portrait depicts William von Covenhoven, a New Jersey Patriot who eventually moved west to settle in Indiana.

IOWA The Iowa Room is furnished as a parlor with well-made furnishings of the eighteenth and early nineteenth centuries. The room also contains a number of interesting portraits including those of Mr. and Mrs. William Young. Their likenesses were painted in Geneva, New York around 1830 and descended in an Iowa branch of the sitters' family. The pair of charcoal portraits on the chimney breast, of an unknown couple, are in the French style.

KANSAS The Kansas Chapel is a scaled-down re-creation of the Sargent Chapel in the Congregational Church in Topeka, Kansas. The stained-glass windows were removed from the 1911 Carnegie Library in Wichita before it was torn down. The sunflower, which grows wild on the Kansas prairies, was adopted as the official state flower in 1903. The chapel suggests the agrarian economy of the state and the religious spirit of its people.

KENTUCKY The furnishings of the Kentucky Room have the lighter proportions of the early neo-classical style. On the walls hang a portrait of Colonel William Piatt, who served with Andrew Jackson at the siege of New Orleans, and an engraving of the Towhe Bunting after a drawing by John James Audubon, a one time resident of Louisville, Kentucky.

LOUISIANA The Louisiana Room is unique among the State Rooms in that it is arranged like a gallery. Among the objects on display which have a distinctly Louisiana feeling are the sofa and two side chairs. In the late neo-classical or Grecian style, they were probably made by French emigré craftsmen working in New Orleans. The painting of Princess Achille Murat, wife of Napoleon Bonaparte's nephew, was painted in New Orleans in 1837.

MAINE   The large needlework family register in the Maine Room records the life dates of members of the John Flint family of Bath, Maine. It was probably worked by a daughter while away at school in Portland. The easy chair, card table, and shelf clock are all of New England origin.

MARYLAND   By the close of the Revolution, Baltimore was the principal Maryland port, and the new prosperity resulting from this increased commercial activity was reflected in the home furnishings of Baltimore residents. Exotic goods, imported directly from China or England, were used side by side with objects shipped down from the northern states and products of local manufacture. Among the latter is the secretary bookcase which belonged to a Baltimore family.

MASSACHUSETTS   The Massachusetts bed chamber was one of the earliest State Rooms
to be furnished in Memorial Continental Hall and was designed after
a room in the Hancock-Clarke home in Concord, Massachusetts. The
maple bedstead and banister-back chairs are probably of New England
origin while the tiles around the fireplace opening were imported
from Holland.

MICHIGAN   Over the fireplace in the Michigan Room hangs the lovely portrait of
Sarah Humes Porter, painted by Jacob Eichholtz. Her husband, George
Bryan Porter, whose portrait also hangs in the room, was named
governor of the Michigan Territory in 1831. A number of the other
furnishings in the room are English in origin and suggest an English
library of the late eighteenth century.

MISSOURI   The Missouri Room represents a Victorian parlor in the second half of the nineteenth century, and the furnishings create an atmosphere of ease and luxury. They include the fashionable gas-lit chandelier, the Aubusson carpet, the imported marble fireplace surround with its ornate overmantel looking glass, the amply-upholstered seating furniture, the elaborately-carved sofa table and the multi-tiered display table laden with decorative objects.

NEW HAMPSHIRE   On June 26, 1928, the New Hampshire State Society voted to purchase a room in Memorial Continental Hall. Then called the "nursery," the name was changed in 1930 to the "Children's Attic" to better describe its decoration as an attic playroom. Wallace Nutting, the noted antiquarian, artist, author, and cabinetmaker from Massachusetts, was hired to design the room. He planned it around an over-mantel painting from a house in Piermont, New Hampshire.

NEW JERSEY   Installed prior to 1911, the New Jersey Room is an embodiment of the antiquarian spirit which gave birth to the DAR Museum in 1890. The panelling and furniture for the room were carved from oak timbers salvaged from the British ship *Augusta*, which sank during the Battle of Red Bank, October 23, 1777. The painted glass windows depict Revolutionary War battles fought in New Jersey, and the portraits are of the five New Jersey Signers of the Declaration of Independence.

NEW YORK   Because of the importance of the China trade to the economy and culture of New York City, a number of accessories in the New York Room are Chinese in origin. The porcelain and the game board were made in the eighteenth and early nineteenth centuries for the Western market, and the wallpaper, handpainted in the traditional manner, was made in Hong Kong in the twentieth century. The sofa, card table and chairs were made in New England and the mid-Atlantic states.

NORTH CAROLINA   The North Carolina Room is furnished as a dining room in an early nineteenth century home. The dining table, sideboard and chairs are American, while the silver épergne and mahogany knife boxes are English in origin. The wallpaper is a later version of "The Hunt," a scenic paper first printed by Zuber and Co. in Alsace in 1831.

OHIO   The Ohio Room, an early nineteenth century parlor, is graced by the portraits of Captain and Mrs. Nathan Haley. The sofa and pianoforte are in the American Empire style and were made in the New York area. The tiger maple work table was made in Ohio and was owned by the Babcock family of Portage County. The Argand lamps beside the sofa are English Sheffield plate, and the ones on the mantle are from Boston.

41

OKLAHOMA   The Oklahoma kitchen was completed in 1931, soon after the crane and brickbats had been purchased from an old house near Media, Pennsylvania. The room is filled with useful domestic and cooking accessories which were once used in homes located across the United States.

PENNSYLVANIA   The Pennslyvania Alcove offers a sampling of the furniture which distinguished Pennsylvania craftsmen in the second half of the eighteenth century, a period when Philadelphia was the recognized cultural and artistic center of the nation.

RHODE ISLAND   The Rhode Island Room is furnished as a music room with a selection of nineteenth century American and European instruments. Learning to play the pianoforte, cello or harp was considered an important part of a genteel education.

SOUTH CAROLINA   The most recently installed State Room suggests an early nineteenth-century bed chamber with its summer textile coverings. The pine fireplace surround was taken from the Carwile-McClentocky House in Edgefield, South Carolina, and the child's bedstead comes from Greenville County.

TENNESSEE   Several objects in the Tennessee State Room relate to the history of the White House. The portrait of Andrew Jackson, the state's most celebrated hero, was painted by his artist friend, Ralph E.W. Earl. It shows him seated in one of the chairs ordered by President Monroe from the French cabinetmaker Pierre Antoine Bellangé in 1817 for the Oval Room in the White House. Displayed below the portrait is one of the gilded armchairs from that set. The pair of mahogany armchairs by the Georgetown cabinetmaker, William King Jr., are from a set of twenty-four chairs and four sofas commissioned by Monroe that same year for the East Room of the White House.

TEXAS   The Texas Bedroom suggests a Texas interior in the German immigrant style of around 1850 to 1880. The inspiration for its decoration came from a bedroom in an extant house located in Alleyton, outside of Columbus, Texas. The wall stenciling was done by artists who specialized in traditional Texas stenciling, and the furnishings are all either of Texas origin or have a history of having been used in the region. Of particular interest is the wardrobe or kleiderschrank, an essential element in the closetless bedroom.

VERMONT   The Vermont Room is furnished as a rural interior of the early nine-
          teenth century. Portraits of Samuel and Lydia Dyer Townsend of
          Wallingford, Vermont flank the sofa. They were painted in 1832 by
          James Whitehorne, a local painter.

VIRGINIA The Virginia Room contains furnishings which might be found in a
          dining room in the Tidewater area of Virginia or Maryland. The
          mahogany dining table and set of six side chairs were made in the
          South, possibly Baltimore, in the Federal period. The table is set with
          porcelain exported to America from the Chinese port of Canton.

WEST VIRGINIA   The West Virginia Room contains a number of objects which can be associated with that area. The pianoforte was made by Charles Taws of Philadelphia and was transported by Henley Chapman from Philadelphia to his home in Giles County, Virginia. The writing desk, once owned by Robert Rutherford, and the Windsor chair were also used in Virginia, in that part of the state that became West Virginia after the Civil War. Above the fireplace hangs a portrait of Dr. Richard Pindell, a surgeon in the First Maryland Regiment.

WISCONSIN   The Wisconsin Room represents a hall or all-purpose room in a seventeenth century New England home. A hall might be used as a kitchen, dining room, sitting-room, bedroom, nursery, office, or schoolroom. Chests, such as this oak and pine "sunflower" chest from the Hartford, Connecticut, region would have held and helped preserve the family linens. The turned oak joint stool could be moved about the room with ease, and the walnut gateleg table could be folded and stored against the wall, thus providing additional space for family activities.

Declaration of Independence—facsimile in silver, greatly enlarged
(5 x 9 feet), at left of entrance lobby, Memorial Continental Hall.
The low relief is the size of John Trumbull's original painting, and
depicts the Drafting Committee. The familiar replica by John Trumbull
of this scene is beneath the Capitol dome in Washington.

47

1776

Administration Building
DAUGHTERS OF
THE AMERICAN REVOLUTION

1949

ENTRANCE
MUSEUM ·
PERIOD · ROOMS
LIBRARY ·
AMERICANA
COLLECTION
OPEN TO THE PUBLIC

Entrance to Administration Building

Administration Building

Barely a decade after completing Memorial Continental Hall, an Administration Building to house the national officers and their clerical staffs was authorized. On June 3, 1921, ground was broken for this building back of Memorial Continental Hall and connected to it by two glass-enclosed corridors separated by a garden. By action of the Fifty-Seventh Continental Congress, the corridors were replaced by the second section of the Administration Building, solidly filling in the space between the first section and Memorial Continental Hall. It was completed and dedicated two years later, on April 18, 1950. The entrance on D Street has the distinctive number of 1776.

The rapid growth of the Society, with the attendant need for more space in which to carry out its work that made it necessary to expand the Administration Building, was also felt by the Museum. In 1950, the collections were moved from Memorial Continental Hall, where they had been housed for forty years, to the first floor of the Administration Building.

The Museum Gallery occupies the center of the building. Along the outside walls are the offices of national officers and their staffs. A recent installation in one room is the Seimes Microfilm Center.

The President General and her staff are in a suite of rooms on the second floor. In addition to offices, there are several special facilities and rooms on this floor. The Americana Room is housed here. Through the courtesy of the National Officers Club, the Historical Research Library is located in their Board Room.

In the center of the second floor, and conveniently accessible for the President General, is the Assembly Room. There are more offices on the third floor.

In 1980, the Administration Building was expanded for the third time, adding eight new offices, four each on the second and third floors, and an atrium.

Martha Washington by E. F. Andrews. This familiar full length portrait, a copy by the artist of his original painting, commissioned by the Congress of the United States, and which hangs in the East Room of the White House, is the focal point of the Martha Washington Gallery.

Mary Lightfoot was painted by John Wollaston when she was seven years old. At age fifteen she married William Allen, owner of large tracts of land in Surry County, Virginia. John Wollaston painted members of a number of prominent families in New York, Maryland and Virginia.

The Museum

A few steps inside the entrance to the National Headquarters complex of buildings is the doorway to the DAR Museum. On the far wall more than 160 feet from that door is the larger-than-lifesize portrait of Martha Washington.

The DAR Museum traces its beginnings to the very month that the National Society, Daughters of the American Revolution was organized. The following motion was passed in October 1890: "That after this Association has assisted in completion of the monument to Mary Washington, the next effort shall be to provide a place for the collection of historical relics which will accumulate at the World's Fair, and for all other relics which may come to the Society, and for historical portraits, pictures, etc. This may first be in rooms, and later in the erection of a fireproof building." That same year a Revolutionary Relics Committee was established to collect, preserve, and exhibit the relics.

The Committee acquired gifts rapidly. These were first housed in the rooms that the Society used as offices in a downtown Washington office building. By 1899, the collection of some fifty items—manuscripts, porcelain, furniture, silver, and pewter—were temporarily deposited at the Smithsonian Institution, as provided in the charter from the United States Congress to the Daughters of the American Revolution in 1896. When Memorial Continental Hall was completed in 1910, the South Gallery, adjacent to the auditorium, provided the Society with an exhibition area in its own "fireproof building." Later the North Gallery became a part of the Museum, doubling the exhibit space. In 1950, when the second section of the Administration Building was built onto Memorial Continental Hall, the Museum Gallery was moved here. It occupies the center of the first floor, extending from Memorial Continental Hall to Constitution Hall. In a special display case dominated by the life-size figure of Caroline Scott Harrison, the first President General of the NSDAR (1890-1892) and the wife of Benjamin Harrison, President of the United States, is a collection reflecting her interests and her talents. Mrs. Harrison's gown, the gift of her grandchildren to the Society, is the one used for her official portrait, which was presented by the DAR to the White House in 1894.

(A copy of this portrait is in the President General's Reception Room in Constitution Hall.)

The Museum Gallery currently presents changing exhibitions of decorative arts made and used in America before 1830. Paintings, furniture, silver, glass, ceramics, and other art objects of the early settlers depict an interesting and attractive history of a growing nation.

The collection includes the portrait of Thomas McKean, a Signer of the Declaration of Independence, as well as the 18th century Philadelphia Chippendale sofa owned by him. Among other portraits are: President Andrew Jackson by Ralph E. W. Earl; Mary Lightfoot by John Wollaston; and the Maryland statesman, Nicholas Harwood, by James Peale, Revolutionary soldier and painter.

The Arts of Independence: The DAR Museum Collection written by Elisabeth Donaghy Garrett, former Director-Curator of the Museum, was published in early 1985. This hard back, beautifully written and illustrated volume is the first publication devoted entirely to the Museum collection and Period Rooms. Many of the Museum's objects are illustrated for the first time; all of the State Period Rooms are included and described.

This Philadelphia reverse curve sofa has a history of ownership by Thomas McKean, a Delaware Signer of the Declaration of Independence.

The teapot, cup and spoons were made by the Patriot and silversmith Paul Revere. Of Huguenot descent, Revere supplied a number of Boston families with silverware while maintaining an active interest in the political affairs of his community.

This handsome Massachusetts side chair descended in the Fessenden family of Lexington, Massachusetts. According to tradition it was given to Nathan Fessenden by John Hancock, following British damage to the Fessenden property during the Battle of Lexington.

Needlework pocketbooks, the handwork of colonial women, were frequently carried by men and used for currency, papers, jewelry and other valuables.

Sybil Ludington, the "female Paul Revere," rode forty miles on horse-back the night of April 26, 1777 to alert the Minutemen of Putnam County, New York. The painting, by Herbert Bohnert, shows the sculptor, Anna Hyatt Huntington, at work on the heroic bronze statue placed near Carmel, on the shore of Lake Glenida. The small statue below it was presented to the DAR by the sculptor.

The changing exhibition area of the Museum provides the opportunity to display objects borrowed from individuals and institutions as well as a variety of different types of objects from the permanent collection. One such exhibition highlighted the needlework accomplishments of nineteenth-century Maryland women.

"The Touch of Independence," a children's discovery area, introduces young museum visitors to objects used or made in America during the time of the American Revolution. "The Touch of Independence" program complements the objects on view in the Museum Gallery and the DAR Museum's Period Rooms. Children are given an opportunity to handle objects in a relaxed learning environment. A recent addition to the discovery area is a collection of child size chairs similar to full scale examples in the Museum collection.

A favorite with members and visitors is the parlor set up in the Museum Gallery with a selection of period furnishings from the permanent collection. At Christmas time, the focal point is a tree trimmed in the Victorian style and surrounded by an intriguing array of nineteenth-century dolls, toys and games.

The Presidents General

Office of the President General at National Headquarters.

DAR Presidents General

1890-92	Mrs. Benjamin Harrison	1913-17	Mrs. William Cumming Story
1893-95	Mrs. Adlai E. Stevenson	1917-20	Mrs. George Thacher Guernsey
1895-96	Mrs. John W. Foster	1920-23	Mrs. George Maynard Minor
1896-98	Mrs. Adlai E. Stevenson	1923-26	Mrs. Anthony Wayne Cook
1898-01	Mrs. Daniel Manning	1926-29	Mrs. Grace L. H. Brosseau
1901-05	Mrs. Charles W. Fairbanks	1929-32	Mrs. Lowell Fletcher Hobart
1905-09	Mrs. Donald McLean	1932-35	Mrs. Russell William Magna
1909-13	Mrs. Matthew T. Scott	1935-38	Mrs. William A. Becker

President General's and Founders' Pins (reduced). The official badge of the President General, with the seal of the Society surrounded by diamonds and sapphires, is worn by each President General while in office. The Founders' pins, presented in 1897 to Eugenia Washington, Mary Desha, Ellen Hardin Walworth, and Mary S. Lockwood (the last named, known as the "Pen Founder," received the Service pin), are on view at National Headquarters.

1938-41	Mrs. Henry M. Robert, Jr.	1965-68	Mrs. William Henry Sullivan, Jr.
1941-44	Mrs. William H. Pouch	1968-71	Mrs. Erwin Frees Seimes
1944-47	Mrs. Julius Y. Talmadge	1971-74	Mrs. Donald Spicer
1947-50	Mrs. Roscoe C. O'Byrne	1974-75	Mrs. Henry Stewart Jones
1950-53	Mrs. James B. Patton	1975-77	Mrs. Wakelee Rawson Smith
1953-56	Miss Gertrude S. Carraway	1977-80	Mrs. George Upham Baylies
1956-59	Mrs. Frederic A. Groves	1980-83	Mrs. Richard Denny Shelby
1959-62	Mrs. Ashmead White	1983-86	Mrs. Walter Hughey King
1962-65	Mrs. Robert V. H. Duncan		

The Atrium

In 1978, the Society authorized creating eight new offices in the 1950 addition to the Administration Building. The Atrium is part of this expansion project.

On the wall are First Day Issue posters of three postage stamps: Philip Mazzei, Dolley Madison, and Touro Synagogue.

The Assembly Room

The Assembly Room on the second floor of the Administration Building.

This room is used by the President General for conferences. It contains many of the objects that were in Memorial Continental Hall when the Hall was used as the Society's auditorium.

The Americana Collection, The Special Collection Pertaining to NSDAR History, and the Archives

The concept of an Americana Room which would house the manuscripts and imprints pertaining to the history of Colonial America, the Revolutionary War period, and the Early Republic emerged at the time of the commemoration of the 50th Anniversary of the NSDAR in 1940. Prior to that time, no formal collection of such material existed at the National Society. Early American manuscript letters, diaries,

Membership Certificate of The Society of the Cincinnati, organized by the officers of the American Army, May 10, 1783. Signed at Mount Vernon on October 31, 1785, "in the Tenth year of the Independence of the United States," by George Washington as President of the Society.

wills, land grants, muster rolls, and sermons, as well as newspapers, almanacs, rare books, pamphlets, and printed paper currency could be found amongst the holdings of the DAR Museum and the DAR Library.

The "Repository of Americana and Historical Documents Pertaining to the American Revolution" founded in 1940 with the intent of

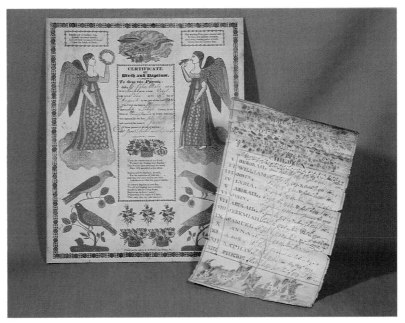

Fraktur paintings, an ornate kind of handwriting developed in the 16th century. One is a birth certificate of Jacob Mohr, born August 19, 1788, and the other is a record of the family of William Bucknam and his wife, Ann, and their thirteen children, 1706-1824.

"Battle of Bennington, August 16, 1777," by Mrs. Anna Mary Robertson Moses (Grandma Moses). The artist, a DAR member, presented the painting to the Society in 1953.

housing all of the above-mentioned materials in one collection is now referred to as the "Americana Collection" of the NSDAR. Today, this ever-expanding collection of about 5,000 historical documents includes such noteworthy items as: a collection of all the signatures of the Signers of the Declaration of Independence (lacking Button Gwinnett), two autograph collections of the Framers of the Constitution of the United States, and a signature and portrait collection focusing on prominent late 18th century foreign statesmen and women (including the Comte de Rochambeau and his son, Vicomte de Rochambeau; King Louis XVI of France; Empress Catherine of Russia; King George III of England; and Pope Pius VI). While predominant emphasis is placed on the American Revolutionary War period and the Early Republic, unusual important material pertaining to subsequent American history and of potential value historically is also included in the Americana Collection. Continuing projects include the gathering of autographs of Presidents of the United States and First Ladies.

The Americana Room

Today the Americana Room is located in the NSDAR Administration Building and serves as the Office of the Historian General. The original location of the room, on the ground floor under the portico honoring the Thirteen Original Colonies on the south side of Memorial Continental Hall, was found to be unsuitable and the collection was moved to its present location on the second floor of the Administration Building after that building was enlarged in 1950. The Americana Room is a handsomely furnished and well-equipped room, including lovely cabinets and display cases, protective lighting, a security system, and special temperature and humidity controls, all designed to provide maximum protection for the collection. (Visitors are welcome during the week, Monday to Friday, 8:30 to 4.)

In the 1960s, and, in particular when the NSDAR celebrated its 75th Anniversary in 1965, collecting memorabilia which relates to the history of the National Society and its Founders has been emphasized. This collection of materials is currently referred to as the Special Collection pertaining to NSDAR history and is housed in the Americana Room. In more recent years, the NSDAR Archives has been formally established with the intent of collecting and preserving the non-current working records of the National Society. The majority of material in the NSDAR Archives is housed in a special, separate room at the National Headquarters.

Seimes Microfilm Center

The Seimes Microfilm Center was established in 1969 to build a resource for genealogical research on film and microfiche. Materials include DAR applications, Federal census, some States censuses, Regional and Family records. Contributions from DAR Chapters and State organizations to the Center are encouraged as Life Memberships, Memorial Tributes or Honorees. The Seimes Microfilm Center is open Monday through Friday 8:30 to 4:00 o'clock. A fee is charged to non-DAR members.

Historical Research Library

The Historical Research Library was established in 1967 to answer queries on the American Revolutionary era and on NSDAR history. The facility contains 1,350 volumes and 150 pamphlets. Free.

Opening Night—Continental Congress

Constitution Hall

Constitution Hall is a "Memorial to that Immortal Document The Constitution of the United States in which are Incorporated those Principles of Freedom, Equality, and Justice for which Our Forefathers Strove. Erected by The National Society Daughters of the American Revolution. Cornerstone Laid October 30, 1928." These words are carved in the cornerstone of Constitution Hall. Mrs. Calvin Coolidge, then First Lady, assisted in laying the stone, and put her card and that of the President inside it. The gavel that was used to tap the stone into place was the same one that George Washington used in laying the cornerstone of the United States Capitol.

The Daughters of the American Revolution were urgently in need of a new and larger auditorium by 1924, having outgrown the auditorium seating 1,666 in their first building, Memorial Continental Hall. That year, the President General of the Society was authorized to secure and submit tentative plans for the erection of an auditorium on the vacant land facing Eighteenth Street. In December, John Russell Pope, New York architect, presented his first plans for the new building, but these were thought to be for a structure that was too large, and too costly. In January, 1925, he submitted a second plan and this was accepted by the Society at its Continental Congress the following April. Pope estimated that the new auditorium building would cost $1,825,000. He arrived at this approximate figure by putting the cost of a cubic foot at $1.00.

Constitution Hall was the first of several structures in the vicinity of The Mall in the Nation's Capital which were designed by John Russell Pope. The others are the American Pharmaceutical Institute Building near the Lincoln Memorial; the National Gallery of Art Building and the National Archives Building, between the Capitol and the White House; and the Jefferson Memorial [1937, the year Pope died] on the axis that crosses The Mall from the White House.

Constitution Hall faces Eighteenth Street between C and D Streets, Northwest, and is a block long and a third of a block deep. The building is constructed of Alabama limestone. It is one of a complex occupying an entire city square that is owned by the Daughters of the American Revolution.

Constitution Hall, one of the largest auditoriums in the world

(4,000 capacity), is noted for its superb acoustics

Excavating for Constitution Hall was begun on August 24, 1928, and the first event held in the Hall, a Vesper Service, took place on October 23, 1929.

The Ionic entrance portico of the building is surmounted by a 90-foot-wide pediment above the name, CONSTITUTION HALL, cut in the stone frieze. The huge sculptured American eagle, and the dates "1776" and "1783" of the Declaration of Independence and the Treaty of Paris, respectively, to the right and left of the eagle, were carved *in situ* by the sculptor, Ulysses A. Ricci. High on the wall under the portico are five-foot-tall allegorical low-relief panels. Below each panel, and between them, are three pairs of bronze doors. Directly above the center doors is a bronze plaque inscribed: "Let us raise a standard to which the wise and honest can repair. The event is in the hands of God. George Washington to the Constitution Convention, A.D. 1787."

A broad flight of steps on this, the main approach to Constitution Hall, leads past the entrance pillars supporting the portico. The building's triple frontage permits entrances on three sides; the approach on C Street is by way of a promenade and that of D Street by a driveway. Within, these entrances are connected by a grand lobby. There are five pairs of bronze doors on each of the two sides of the building plus the three pairs on the front, the total representative of the thirteen original colonies.

The spacious lobby leads into the great U-shaped auditorium, which is surrounded by 52 boxes, their facades decorated with the various State seals. Custom-designed and specially woven material of gold medallions and stars on a blue background, with an elaborately woven border of gold eagles surrounded by garlands, was used for the 25-foot-long stage curtains. The medallion and star motif is repeated in the vinyl wall-covering on the front of the boxes and exit walls around the entire auditorium. The hard surface on these walls, and on the floor, was chosen for acoustical reasons.

On either side of the stage are graceful twin Ionic columns, each topped by a 3½-foot American Bald Eagle finished in 14-carat gold leaf. Centered above the stage is a painted lunette of the Great Seal of the United States, flanked by twelve Revolutionary flags. Under the Seal are the names of the thirteen original colonies in geographical order. Inconspicuouly lodged at the foot of the stage is the three-manual Skinner organ's console. Backstage are dressing rooms and the Conductor's Room.

A marble stairway, lighted by day by a large decorative bronze window of exceptional beauty, leads to the second floor of Constitution Hall. The Genealogical Library, which it was intended to house, quickly outgrew this space. A large meeting room and offices of the Children of the American Revolution occupy the north and south ends, respectively. The central area is now used to exhibit a collection of decorative and applied arts for children and young adults. It is one

Located in the northeast corner of Constitution Hall, with doors to the lobby and a passageway to the stage, this lovely and spacious formal room is used by the President General for receiving members and guests. The portrait of Mrs. Benjamin Harrison, First President General of the Daughters of the American Revolution at the time she was First Lady, is a copy by Mathilde Leisenring in 1931 of the one by Daniel Huntington that the Daughters presented to the White House in 1894. The room's predominant colors are golden beige and crimson. The sofa was a gift from Dr. John W. Scott, Mrs. Harrison's father, to the Society.

of the few such displays in Washington. Open to the public, it is free.

The Daughters' initial purpose in building Constitution Hall had been to provide seating for the delegates to the Society's annual meetings. But even before the first of these meetings took place in April, 1930, the Hall had been used for concerts, lectures, and other cultural events connected with the performing arts. At the laying of the cornerstone, the Honorable Charles Moore, Chairman of the National Commission of Fine Arts, made this prediction: "For the highest form of music, the symphony concert, this auditorium will make suitable and adequate provisions. It may lead to a permanent orchestra. You may make it a platform for the world's thinkers, as well as a place to honor men of achievements." All these predictions became realities immediately after the hall was completed.

On November 2, 1931, the first concert ever of the National Symphony Orchestra, with Hans Kindler, founder of the orchestra, conducting, took place in Constitution Hall. The Hall was the "home" of the National Symphony Orchestra for more than forty years.

The Hall has been the "home" of the National Geographic Society's lecture series for more than half a century. The regular season series of lectures started in 1933-1934 but there were special lectures before then. The National Geographic Society has given a total of some 2,000 lectures in Constitution Hall. Nestled high in the ceiling of the auditorium, behind the west balcony, are 16mm and 35mm motion picture sound projectors and spot lights. The stage curtains hide a portable motion picture screen.

Although Constitution Hall was built for the Daughters annual Continental Congress, it quickly became the cultural center for the Nation's Capital and a nationally and internationally known focus for all forms of the performing and literary arts. It has retained much of its importance in Washington's cultural life despite the construction of the Kennedy Center. Today the Daughters rent the Hall as a service to the people in the District of Columbia and the surrounding metropolitan areas. Because the Daughters of the American Revolution have made their buildings a constituent part of the National Capital plan, Constitution Hall has a national significance. It was designated a National Historic Landmark Building in 1985.

PART II

The Story of the Daughters

73 THE FOUNDERS

75 HISTORICAL, EDUCATIONAL, AND
    PATRIOTIC PURSUITS

90 AN OVERVIEW, 1890 & 1986

94 MAJOR NATIONAL AND INTERNATIONAL
    GIFTS OR COMMEMORATIONS

Sculptor: Gertrude Vanderbilt Whitney

The Founders

The marble memorial honoring the Four Founders of the Daughters of the American Revolution, in a beautiful garden setting on C Street, N.W., between Memorial Continental Hall and Constitution Hall, was dedicated on April 17, 1929. The single nine-foot-high figure, with flowing drapery and outstretched arms, symbolizes American womanhood. The Founders are separately honored by engraved bronze medallions located on the long horizontal monument which forms the background for the statue.

The inscription reads:

> TO THE WOMEN WHOSE PATRIOTIC
> FORESIGHT MADE POSSIBLE
>
> THE NATIONAL SOCIETY
> DAUGHTERS OF THE AMERICAN
> REVOLUTION

and the founding date October 11, 1890.

Eugenia Washington (1840-1900), holder of National Number One, served as one of the two first Registrars General, who jointly held office at that time. Later she was Recording Secretary General, Vice President General, and Honorary Vice President General. Affectionately called "Miss Eugie," Miss Washington was a modest and retiring person. Although suffering from a serious eye condition that made writing difficult, she diligently carried out the duties of her office.

We want a patriotic society founded on service and I will not become a member of an organization which is founded on rank and not on the service of the ancestors.

Mary Desha (1850-1911) was a Vice President General of the newly formed Society. (The family name had originally been DuChene, but at this time was pronounced "Deshay," with the accent on the last syllable.)

It was Miss Desha who suggested the design for the Society's Seal of a dame sitting at her spinning wheel as a suitable companion to the man at the plow.

Miss Desha was also Surgeon General, Corresponding Secretary General, Recording Secretary General, and Honorary Vice President General. Her standard of action as a Daughter was the Constitution of the Society and she would not permit the slightest departure from it.

I want the ladies to vote, but I want it to go on record that I wish to adhere to the strict letter of the Constitution.

Ellen Hardin Walworth (1832-1915) was the first Corresponding Secretary General. She was also a Vice President General and Honorary Vice President General. Mrs. Walworth was president and founder of the Art and Science Field Club of Saratoga (New York): it was she who suggested that the Society present a portrait of Mrs. Benjamin Harrison to the White House. Mrs. Walworth was by authorization of the Board of Management of May 7, 1892, editor of the Society's Magazine.

That the Board of Management publish a monthly magazine, which shall contain the report of the proceedings of the Continental Congress, and from time to time, the proceedings of the Board of Management, and such reports as may be sent from the respective Chapters, all to be under the charge of Mrs. Ellen Hardin Walworth, subject to the supervision of the Board.

Mary Smith Lockwood (1831-1922), the "Pen Founder" of the Society, was its first Historian General. She was also Chaplain General, Surgeon General, Assistant Historian General (later Reporter General to the Smithsonian Institution), Vice President General, and Honorary Vice President General. A small, slight but extremely energetic woman, she was the author of several books and a member of the National Press Association. Although the oldest of the Founders, she was the last survivor among them. It is Mrs. Lockwood who is credited with having spoken the first words in behalf of Memorial Continental Hall, in a motion she introduced at the second organizational meeting on October 18, 1890.

That after this Association has assisted in the completion of the monument of Mary Washington, the next effort shall be to provide a place for the collection of Historical relics. . . . This may first be in rooms, and later in the erection of a fireproof building.

All the Founders were single women at the time of their service to the Society: Miss Desha and Miss Washington had never married; Mrs. Walworth and Mrs. Lockwood were widows. The four were similarly grouped geographically: the first two came from the South, the last two from the North. In at least two other ways the four were alike: as unmarried women, or as widows, all were self-supporting, working women and all were dedicated to the Society they had founded.

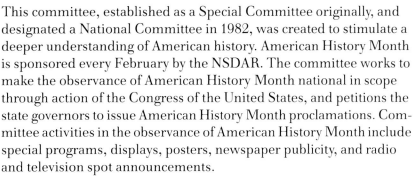

Historical, Educational, and Patriotic Pursuits

The National Society, Daughters of the American Revolution carries on its work through committees. The pages that follow summarize these committee activities. (The date when each committee was established is indicated in parentheses.)

AMERICAN HERITAGE (1963)

Created to aid and encourage the preservation, appreciation and promotion for the future of our rich American heritage in arts, crafts, drama and literature, and music. The Evelyn Cole Peters Certificate is awarded for outstanding achievement in this field. In addition, certificates are given in the four individual categories.

AMERICAN HISTORY MONTH (1956)

This committee, established as a Special Committee originally, and designated a National Committee in 1982, was created to stimulate a deeper understanding of American history. American History Month is sponsored every February by the NSDAR. The committee works to make the observance of American History Month national in scope through action of the Congress of the United States, and petitions the state governors to issue American History Month proclamations. Committee activities in the observance of American History Month include special programs, displays, posters, newspaper publicity, and radio and television spot announcements.

This committee encourages the study of American history in all grades of school and each year conducts an American History Essay Contest for the 5th, 6th, 7th and 8th grades. Medals and certificates are awarded.

Beginning in 1981, with the cooperation of the office of the Historian General, the National Society annually recognizes an Outstanding Teacher of American History.

AMERICANISM AND DAR MANUAL FOR CITIZENSHIP (1919)

The goal of this committee is better citizenship. It stresses educating native-born and naturalized Americans to be aware of the privileges and responsibilities of American citizenship.

The *DAR Manual for Citizenship*, originally printed in seventeen languages but now only in English, is given free to those studying to become naturalized citizens and is made available to others. Over ten million copies have been distributed since 1921. DAR members attend naturalization courts and distribute United States flags to new citizens.

In Washington, DAR interest in this work began early in the century with Italian immigrants who had come to the capital city to work on building the railroad station. By 1913, DAR members were holding citizenship classes for foreign-born in a back room of a small store in Georgetown. Mainly through their efforts, the Congress of the United States authorized Federal funds to found the Americanization School, the only one of its kind in the country. This school is now a part of the District of Columbia educational system.

The Americanism and DAR Manual for Citizenship Committee awards a number of medals, pins and certificates. The most prized among them, and given to non-DAR members only, are the Americanism Award and the Medal of Honor.

Qualifications for both the Americanism Award and the Medal of Honor are exceedingly high; all recipients must show leadership, trustworthiness, and patriotism. A fourth qualification is service. In this area the requirements for the awards differ. A proposed recipient for the Americanism Award—an adult naturalized citizen who has been a United States citizen for at least five years and fulfilled the required qualifications following naturalization—must have actively assisted other aliens to become American citizens, OR, outstandingly participated in community affairs with emphasis on the foreign-born community, if possible. The Medal of Honor is awarded to an adult native-born citizen; this recipient must have given outstanding service which has contributed to the betterment of the community.

AMERICAN INDIANS (1941)

Originally authorized as a subcommittee in 1936 "to help first Americans first," it was established as a National Committee five years later. Its purpose is to aid and support the education of Indian youth. Bacone College in Muskogee, Oklahoma, is emphasized in the Society's work with American Indians. Contributions include scholarships.

BICENTENNIAL OF THE CONSTITUTION OF THE U.S.A. (1984)

A Special Committee called the Bicentennial of the Constitution of the United States of America Committee has been appointed to commemorate the 200th anniversary of the greatest document ever conceived by the mind of man. A special Vice Chairman was appointed to the Constitution Week Committee to serve as liaison for this committee.

CENTENNIAL JUBILEE, NSDAR (1982)

This Special Committee was created for the purpose of observing the celebration of the 100th Anniversary of the Founding of the NSDAR. October 11, 1990 to October 11, 1991 has been designated for programs, activities and celebrations commemorating this important milestone in the Society's history.

CHILDREN OF THE AMERICAN REVOLUTION (1954)

The National Society, Children of the American Revolution was founded in 1895 by Harriett M. Lothrop (Mrs. Daniel). A committee for the Children of the American Revolution was authorized by the Sixty-Third DAR Continental Congress. The N.S.C.A.R. is a separate organization, incorporated under the laws of the District of Columbia the year it was founded. The current membership is approximately 10,500. Boys and girls may be members in the C.A.R. from birth until their twenty-second birthday.

The C.A.R. has a two-fold purpose: to inculcate a knowledge and appreciation of America's past in our youth so that they can apply the experiences of history to the problems of the present and to train C.A.R. members in leadership and patriotism. Members of parent organizations—Daughters of the American Revolution, Sons of the American Revolution, and Sons of the Revolution—serve as Senior Leaders for these young people.

The N.S.C.A.R. national headquarters and museum are located on the second floor of Constitution Hall.

CONSERVATION (1909)

As its title implies, this committee's aim is to preserve and improve our environment as well as support good legislation in this field. It stresses the need to conserve our natural resources. In the beginning, this committee concentrated on planting trees and protecting wildlife. Each year, the committee still plants many thousands of trees, bulbs and shrubs, and supplies tons of birdseed and wildlife food, and preserves fisheries, wetlands and dunes. But its activities have now been expanded to include acute energy problems and new energy alternatives. Today, the committee's interest in conservation covers not only reforestation and wildlife but also energy and minerals, insect control, planting of windbreaks, multiple use of forests and promoting urban greenbelts to assure green areas around and within cities.

CONSTITUTION WEEK (1955)

This observance was suggested by the DAR early in 1955. In June of that year, a Senate Concurrent Resolution authorized and requested the President of the United States to proclaim Constitution Week and the next year a Senate Joint Resolution was passed to have the President proclaim September 17-23 *every* year as Constitution Week. DAR efforts in behalf of Constitution Week were so outstanding that the National Society received one of the five top special awards from Freedoms Foundation at Valley Forge for this accomplishment.

Each year DAR activities during the week-long celebration increase markedly. Chapters participate by asking governors, mayors and the general public, assisted by all the news media, to cooperate in promoting Constitution Week.

DAR FAMILY TREE GENETICS (1984)

The DAR Family Tree Genetics Project was initiated by the NSDAR to offer an opportunity for each DAR member to share information on health problems within her extended family in an effort to improve the health of present and future generations. The project will trace the health histories within DAR member pedigrees to detect possible patterns of genetic disorders and identify families at risk of hereditary illnesses. Vanderbilt University Medical Center, Nashville, Tennessee, is assisting the NSDAR with this project.

DAR GOOD CITIZENS (1934)

The aim of this committee is to stress the importance of the qualities of good citizenship. All students who are seniors and citizens of the United States attending accredited high schools or high schools approved by the State Board of Education, both public and private, and senior students in American schools in foreign countries, are eligible to participate in this program. The program has the approval of the National Association of Secondary School Principals. A competitive method of selection is used and the candidates are chosen by their classmates and the faculty. The Good Citizen is chosen on a merit basis and must possess the qualities of dependability, service (at school, in the community and at home), leadership and patriotism. Each state winner receives a $100 U.S. Savings Bond and a pin from the National Society, DAR. The Society awards the national winner with a $1,000 scholarship to be applied toward the tuition at the college or university chosen by the contestant, and also presents a sterling silver engraved Paul Revere bowl. Approximately ten thousand schools participate in this program annually.

DAR MAGAZINE (1892)

Shortly after the First Continental Congress in 1892, at a meeting of the Board of Management of the Society on the 7th of May, the following resolution was passed: "That the Board of Management publish a monthly magazine which shall contain the report of the proceedings of the Continental Congress, and from time to time the proceedings of the Board of Management and such reports as may be sent from the respective Chapters, ..." Two months later, *The American Monthly Magazine*, the forerunner of the official magazine of today, came out, with Mrs. E. H. Walworth, one of the Founders of the Society, as editor. Published continuously since July, 1892, it may very well be the oldest periodical of its kind in the world.

In reporting on the Magazine before the Congress of Representative Women in Chicago, Illinois, on May 19, 1893, Mrs. Walworth said: "Just one year ago this month a motion was adopted . . . to publish a magazine. . . . It started without a subscriber, without an advertiser, without a dollar appropriated for its own existence—depending on that which was provided to print the proceedings of the first Continental Congress . . . ."

As the official publication of the Society, the Magazine provides means of communication between national headquarters and the membership. At first, for reasons of economy, both the Minutes of the National Board of Management and the Proceedings of the Continental Congress were published in the Magazine. However, this did not prove practical for as the Society grew, and the field for distribution of the Magazine widened, it became necessary to recognize the demand for other articles and features consistent with the objectives of the Society. So the Nineteenth Congress voted to publish the Congress Proceedings in a separate volume, properly indexed, as soon as possible after the adjournment of Congress. From that time on the Congress Proceedings have been done separately while the Minutes of the National Board continue to be published in the Magazine. It also contains reports of national chairmen and national, state, and chapter news: each issue carries a message from the President General to the members.

During the first two years of the Magazine's existence the subscription price was $1.00 per year with individual copies selling for 20¢. In March, 1893, subscriptions were raised to $2.00 per year. This price prevailed for more than seventy years, until December, 1964, when it was set at $3.00. In May, 1974, in view of rising prices and publication costs, the subscription price was raised to $5.00 per year and individual copies of current issues to 75¢ plus postage.

Both production and postage increased in June, 1981, and the annual subscription price became $7.00.

Recognizing the need for a genealogical index of the *DAR Magazine*, this indexing was undertaken in 1985. The completed project containing more than 1.5 million entries will be a useful tool for genealogists.

DAR MAGAZINE ADVERTISING (1950)

Because of its special interests, the *DAR Magazine* provides an exceptional advertising medium. State and chapter organizations are asked to seek appropriate advertising sponsors. Advertisements of historic places, shrines and sites are encouraged, thus emphasizing the historical, educational and patriotic aspects of each locality. All advertising is subject to the approval of the Society.

DAR MEMBERSHIP COMMISSION (1965)

This committee was established to direct a coordinated program for increasing the membership of the National Society. Its aim is an expanding membership composed of alert and dedicated women who will carry out the objectives of the Society now and in the future.

DAR MUSEUM (1890)

This is the Society's oldest committee. It actually pre-dates the formal organizational date of the Society.

On August 17, 1890, a notice appeared in *The Washington Post* which proposed the founding of a society whose purpose would be to "gather materials for history, to preserve souvenirs of the Revolution, to study the manners and measures of those days, to devise the best methods of perpetuating the memories of our ancestors and celebrating their achievements." To preserve souvenirs of the Revolution was a foremost factor in the founding of the National Society of the Daughters of the American Revolution, and even before the first formal meeting, on October 11, 1890, the founding members had set a goal, "to collect and preserve historical and biographical records, documents and relics." One week later, at a second organizational meeting, it was resolved to "provide a place for the collection of historical relics . . . This may first be in rooms, and later in the erection of a fire-proof building." A Revolutionary Relics Committee was formed: in 1936, the name was changed to DAR Museum Committee.

In the intervening years, the material had grown into an important decorative arts collection, with special emphasis on the Revolutionary War Period of the late eighteenth century.

This committee coordinates the efforts of all Museum related committees (Friends of the Museum, Museum Docents, Art Critics) and includes acquisition, conservation, restoration, preservation, publicizing, and maintaining the Museum and the State Period Rooms.

Two Vice Chairmen assist the Chairman in promoting the Museum. For events sponsored by the Museum, such as the opening of exhibits and commemorations related to the Museum, there is a Vice Chairman in Charge of Special Events. The Vice Chairman in Charge of Correspondent Docents works with members in the various states to present programs on the Museum for DAR chapters and other organizations.

The outstanding collection of American decorative arts in the Museum Gallery and the State Period Rooms totals some 50,000 objects. Tremendous growth of the holdings has been due largely to the generous gifts of members and friends. The Museum special events and children's educational programs have brought many new people to the DAR Museum where they enjoy viewing the treasures preserved there. In 1973, the Museum was accredited by the American Association of Museums.

DAR PATRIOT INDEX (1966)

Authorized in 1966, this committee published the *DAR Patriot Index* the following year. Volume II, published in 1980, contained newly established data along with the entire contents of the three paperback supplements issued between 1967 and 1980. In 1982, another paperback supplement was published. These books are compiled from the information in the records of the National Society giving the names, data, and service of 117,744 patriots whose service has been used to establish the eligibility of DAR members. The third volume of the series, an *Index to the Spouses of the DAR Patriots*, will be published in 1986.

DAR SCHOLARSHIP (1923)

The purpose of this committee, established as the Student Loan & Scholarship Committee and changed in 1979 to the DAR Scholarship Committee, is to provide ways and means to aid worthy, ambitious students to attain higher education by awarding scholarships: Educational, i.e. Political Science, History, Government or Economics; Nursing; and Occupational Therapy.

Annually, through this committee, the NSDAR awards scholarships totaling approximately $60,000. Notable among them are the $8,000 American History Scholarship, $2,000 per year for four years, to a qualifying senior in a high school graduating class; the Lillian and Arthur Dunn Scholarships of $1,000 for four years to six sons or daughters of active DAR members; and the Enid Hall Griswold

Memorial Scholarship of $1,000 each year to a junior or senior student majoring in Political Science, History, Government or Economics.

Since 1908, when the National Society presented a sword to that year's outstanding graduate of the United States Naval Academy, DAR awards have been given to honor graduates of the five service academies and three other military schools annually.

DAR SCHOOL (1903)

As early as 1903, the NSDAR established a Patriotic Education Committee. By 1932, the work covered had increased so much that it was divided into three parts, one of which was called Approved Schools. In 1960, this name was changed to DAR School Committee. The committee is responsible for DAR projects in the two schools in which the National Society has an ownership interest: Tamassee DAR School and Kate Duncan Smith DAR School, plus four Approved Schools.

Tamassee, located at Tamassee, South Carolina, is the first DAR school, founded in 1919 by the South Carolina Daughters. It was made a project of National DAR in 1920. Tamassee, coeducational, is both a boarding and day school for elementary classes—grades 4 through 6, plus kindergarten for pre-school children. Enrollment in 1984 was approximately 87 boarding students and 169 day students. Boarding students are carefully selected on basis of need. Students in grades K-3 and grades 7-12 attend nearby community public schools. Tamassee

Kate Duncan Smith DAR School students.

recently opened a pre-school day care center for the children of Oconee County, South Carolina.

Many extracurricular activities are stressed; some are home economics, arts and crafts, music, and folk dancing.

Kate Duncan Smith DAR School of Grant, Alabama, was established in 1924 by the Alabama Daughters. Grades 1 through 12 plus kindergarten class for pre-school children are taught in the Day School. Enrollment is in excess of 1,000. A special education program has proven very beneficial to the student with learning disabilities. An experienced, qualified teacher in this field has been assigned KDS by the Marshall County Board of Education. In addition to required subjects, the curriculum includes home economics, music, arts and crafts, industrial arts and commercial subjects, including typing and bookkeeping.

An "Agri-business" teacher is teaching horticulture and related

Tamassee DAR School students.

topics to both boys and girls, plus a program in land judging (agriculture) for future farmers. This is part of the Future Farmers of America program in Alabama.

Athletics continue to be an important part of extracurricular activities, especially basketball, baseball, tennis and girls' volleyball.

At each DAR School much of the daily maintenance and repairs are done with the assistance of student labor before and after school and on week-ends. Working scholarships provide payments for this work.

Both schools receive financial assistance from county and/or state for basic teachers' salaries and pupil transportation. For other expenses they depend entirely on DAR for support. In addition to contributions received from chapters and individuals, the National Society gives to each of these schools $30,000 annually. Each school is accredited by the Southern Association of Colleges and Secondary Schools, and the State Department of Education in their respective states.

An "Approved School" is one that has been endorsed by the state DAR where located and approved by the Continental Congress. To qualify for DAR support, a school or college must be for boys and girls who otherwise might not have the opportunity for an education.

It was resolved by Congress in 1940 that as vacancies occurred in the list of Approved Schools, new schools should not be added.

There are currently four Approved Schools:

Berry College, at Mount Berry, Ga., was founded by Miss Martha Berry in 1902. Miss Berry, a member of the DAR, told the delegates at the 13th Continental Congress in 1904 about her school, then in a log cabin. This school became the first to be placed on the approved school list. Berry College is co-educational. The institution's beautiful campus is probably the largest college campus in the world.

Crossnore School, Crossnore, N.C., was established in 1911 as a one-room schoolhouse. The first boarding students were eight girls, who lived in the attic of the teacher's cottage and five boys, who slept in a grist mill loft. Ten years later the school was added to the DAR approved list. Besides providing a home for the students, supplementary educational programs are offered.

Hillside School, in Marlborough, Mass., dates from 1901. It provides year-round care for worthy boys needing a boarding home and school. A traditional course of academic study is offered in grades three to eight during the school year, and there is also a summer camp program.

In 1902, Hindman Settlement School, in Hindman, Ky., was established as a rural educational social center. It contributes significantly to education in the area. Its library serves the high school and the community. A fairly recent addition to its educational program is a musicmobile, which is specifically related to the folk music wealth of the region.

DAR SERVICE FOR VETERAN-PATIENTS (1968)

This committee was created as a Special Committee in 1968 and established as a National Committee in 1972.

The NSDAR is represented on the National Advisory Board of the Veterans Administration Voluntary Service by three members. DAR members are serving in over a 175 medical facilities: one DAR representative and up to three deputy representatives coordinate the work in each hospital. Among the diversified activities in which the DAR engage are giving thousands of hours of volunteer service, hosting parties, donating books and other gifts, collecting hundreds of pounds of cancelled stamps for the "Stamps for the Wounded" program, presenting Braille Flags to blind veterans and performing many personal services. In 1983, an annual Outstanding Veteran-Patient Award was authorized.

DAR SPEAKERS STAFF (1966)

Area representatives of this committee are available to give programs on a variety of subjects and to talk about the past accomplishments and the future aims and purposes of the NSDAR.

FLAG OF THE UNITED STATES OF AMERICA (1909)

The purpose of this committee is to encourage a strong patriotic feeling and respect for the Flag. An important objective is to educate children and adults in the correct use and proper display of the Flag in accordance with the Flag Code adopted by the Congress of the United States. Distributing Flag Codes, initiating programs to make all Americans flag-conscious, and presenting Flags to new citizens at naturalization courts, schools, youth organizations and similar groups are among the activities of this committee.

One of the most active efforts of this committee is the making and distributing of Braille Flags.

FRIENDS OF THE MUSEUM (1956)

A Friends of the Museum Committee was begun in 1956 to provide an opportunity for interested members and friends to contribute to a Museum Acquisitions Fund. The committee was established as a Special Committee in 1962 and functions as support for the Museum.

GENEALOGICAL RECORDS (1913)

The main function of this committee is to copy, index, and prepare in proper form, bind and place in the DAR Library information of genealogical value from unpublished sources such as family Bibles, gravestones, court records, etc. As a result, the DAR Library has assembled a tremendous amount of material not available anywhere else. Researchers, historians and the general public as well as DAR members benefit from this unique service.

HONOR ROLL (1953)

The Honor Roll is a stimulus to chapters and individual members to accomplish certain specified goals each year in order to maintain a well-rounded, annual program promoting all aspects of DAR activity. Recognition is given chapters achieving the required goals. This competition brings splendid results.

INSIGNIA (1891)

The aim of this committee is to give timely and correct information on ordering, wearing, printing, and disposing of the Insignia of the Society.

Early in 1891, the question of deciding upon a badge for the Society arose. A design by Dr. James Brown Goode of the Smithsonian Institution (he was a member of the NSDAR Advisory Board and his wife was Chairman of the Committee on Insignia) was accepted. The design had been suggested to Dr. Goode by his grandmother's spinning wheel, now in the DAR Museum. There was correspondence with several jewelers about making the badge. Caldwell & Company of Philadelphia offered to assume the expense of making the dies for any design chosen by the Society, and to pay the cost of registering the patent of the design. Inasmuch as the fledgling Society's funds were very limited, the liberal offer was accepted. The Philadelphia concern, now J.E. Caldwell Co., has been the official jeweler of the DAR ever since.

JUNIOR AMERICAN CITIZENS (1906)

The work of this committee is for the benefit of children of all races and creeds. Its scope is from kindergarten through high school. Its purposes are to teach good citizenship, (the privileges and responsibilities), loyalty to the United States, respect for the U.S.A. Flag and the history of our country and its government. This is done through the formation of clubs. A JAC Club may be established where there is leadership and wherever interested children can meet together; i.e., schools, orphanages, community centers, neighborhood groups, etc. Membership is free.

Contests and awards are popular aspects of any JAC program. Necessary supplies, literature and member pins are furnished free by the NSDAR.

Junior American Citizens Award (Thatcher Pin) presented to JAC members for outstanding service and good citizenship.

JUNIOR MEMBERSHIP (1937)

This committee is composed of DAR members ages 18 through 35. The goals of this committee are to gain new Junior Members, build a well-informed Junior Membership, encourage active participation in all phases of DAR work, and support the National Junior Membership fund-raising project, the Helen Pouch Memorial Fund.

The Helen Pouch Memorial Fund provides scholarships, medical aid, and general financial assistance to the two DAR schools, Tamassee and Kate Duncan Smith. The Junior Bazaar Booth at the annual national Continental Congress and many state conferences is an important fund-raising means for this project. Monies raised by the Juniors have been used to build the Junior Membership Library at Kate Duncan Smith DAR School and to establish the Arts and Crafts Center at Tamassee DAR School, reflecting the emphasis of the National Society on education.

The National Outstanding Junior Member Contest was initiated in 1963 to give recognition to the achievements of these young women.

LINEAGE RESEARCH (1961)

The purpose of this committee is to assist potential members, through DAR chapters, with free genealogical service when needed to complete their application papers. Such assistance is of vital necessity to the continued growth of the Society. The current interest in family genealogy—it is said to rank in popularity immediately after stamp and coin collecting as a hobby—plus the desire to establish a personal relationship with our Nation's beginnings is reflected in the workload of this committee. A Lineage Research Kit containing instructive material is available to anyone at a nominal price.

MEMBERSHIP (1934)

The work of this committee was originally under the direction of the Registrar General, when it was known as the National Registrar's Committee. In 1934, the National Membership Committee was created.

The membership records date from 1890 and show a constant growth. As a result, there are more than 212,000 active members.

As liaison between the DAR and potential new members, this committee carries a great responsibility to present the National Society creditably, emphasizing its many-faceted activities in the fields of history, education and patriotism. Genealogical Seminars and Lineage Workshops elicit enthusiastic response from prospective members. The committee interests potential members in joining, helps them obtain necessary data and sees to the proper completion of application papers before being submitted to National Headquarters.

MOTION PICTURE (1903), RADIO (1928), TELEVISION (1974)

This committee endeavors to secure better films, radio, and television programs in local communities by establishing a line of pleasant communications with the theatres and television stations.

MUSEUM DOCENTS (1971)

The Museum Docent Committee was authorized in 1971 as a Special Committee. Members who reside in the Washington area train to serve as Docents to provide tours of the State Period Rooms and the Museum Gallery to walk-in visitors and to groups of adults and school children by pre-arrangement. These volunteers also assist with Museum Special Events and contribute to projects supporting the Museum.

NATIONAL DEFENSE (1926)

This committee was established to assist members in carrying out patriotic, historical and educational purposes and at the same time promote the enlightenment of public opinion.

The NSDAR inherently stands for adequate defense of the Nation. Further, it strives to encourage the preservation of our priceless heritage, protection of the Constitution and the free enterprise system, and the upholding of the precepts and ideals of a Democracy in a Republic.

This committee provides an article for the *DAR Magazine* monthly and also for a number of years has published *The National Defender* each month for members and subscribers. The committee alerts the members, and through them the general public, of possible threats to our country's security.

The importance of this committee is reflected in the Honor Roll requirement that each chapter on its meeting agenda shall allow at least five minutes for a National Defense report.

Good Citizenship Medal awarded by National Defense Committee to boys or girls in elementary, junior and senior high schools (public, private and parochial) who fulfill the qualities of honor, service, courage, leadership and patriotism.

ROTC Medal, also presented by National Defense Committee, is awarded to high school and college graduating students who have demonstrated qualities of dependability and good character, adherence to military discipline, leadership ability, and a fundamental and patriotic understanding of the importance of ROTC training.

PROGRAM (1903)

This committee maintains a library of manuscript, 35mm slide, and cassette programs for the purpose of assisting chapters plan their programs to promote the historical, educational, and patriotic objectives of the National Society. These programs are also suitable for schools and other organizations. An updated Program Outline Guide is prepared annually for the guidance of chapters in connection with their yearbooks for the following year. Awards are made during the Continental Congress. Chapters are urged to assist the Program Committee in adding new material to the collection. Program material is available at nominal rental fees.

PROGRAM REVIEWING (1958)
This committee receives, studies and evaluates original material on topics of general interest sent in by chapters. These papers, skits, playlets, and radio and television scripts are listed in a Program Catalogue and made available for chapter use.

PUBLIC RELATIONS (1905)
The purpose of this committee is to tell the public of the historical, educational and patriotic programs and projects of the DAR. Instructions on preparing press releases—the Who, What, Where, When, and How of presenting factual information—are made available. Members participate on radio and television programs that promote the NSDAR objectives. State press books are compiled and judged for the annual Press Book Contest.

SEIMES MICROFILM CENTER (1970)
This facility was established to aid the staff of the National Society verify application papers, to help prospective members establish lineage, and to afford the general public an opportunity to pursue the increasingly popular hobby of searching for their ancestors.

STATUE OF LIBERTY RESTORATION (1984)
This Special Committee was authorized in April, 1984 to promote the restoration of the Statue of Liberty and raise funds for this purpose. The Statue of Liberty, constructed in France, and its pedestal, built in the United States, were funded by private citizens. The restoration project, targeted for completion in 1986, the Statue's 100th birthday, is being financed in the same way.

TRANSPORTATION AND SAFETY (1913)
Originally known as the Railroad Committee, this committee's official title became the Transportation and Safety Committee in 1980. The committee promotes two programs: Transportation and Traffic Safety. Transporting members to meetings results in improved attendance and increased interest in DAR activities. In promoting Traffic Safety, it cooperates in local and national campaigns to improve safety standards and frequently receives recognition for its fine accomplishments. Often this committee is in charge of arranging bus trips to State, District meetings and to Continental Congress.

An Overview, 1890 & 1986

When the National Society, Daughters of the American Revolution was organized in 1890, George Washington's birthday was selected as the date for its annual meeting, the Continental Congress.

In February 1892, leading newspapers announced the upcoming first Congress of the Society in glowing terms:

The most important event in the social world of the capital next week will be the First Annual Continental Congress of the Daughters of the American Revolution. The society is national in scope and personnel and has in its membership, after but a single year's growth, 1200 of the female descendants of the best blood of the men and women who fought and worked in the eight years' struggle for American Independence. The society has about 300 members in Washington, beginning with Mrs. Harrison, president, and running through every branch of official life and every sphere of social activity.

It will be interesting to the lady readers of the [*Philadelphia*] *Inquirer* to give a few interesting details of how the ladies of the Continental Congress propose to occupy their time during their three days' session. The entire affair has been arranged and will be carried out by the distinguished daughters of revolutionary sires without the aid of masculine interference for debasing women's rights, and has for its object the perpetuation of the memories of the deeds of heroic valor of the men and heroic sacrifice and cooperation of the women in the struggle which changed and ennobled the destiny of the human race. . . .

The First Continental Congress was held February 22-24 in the Church of Our Father at 13th and L Streets, Washington, D.C. On foot and in carriages, their badges fluttering in the breeze under a sunny sky, members of the Society and guests made their way over the dry but not dusty streets of the Nation's capital. Badges had been available at the office of the Society, 1505 Pennsylvania Avenue, Room 10, second floor, since the previous week, but the Committee on Credentials was at the church early the opening morning of the Congress for the convenience of regents and delegates. The Washington Mandolin, Banjo and Guitar Club was stationed in the gallery of the flag and flower decorated building.

In the crowded-to-overflowing church (it had a capacity of about 700 and there were some 300 members living in Washington), the President General, Mrs. Benjamin Harrison, took her place beneath the large, two-foot-across replica of the blue and white rosette button of the Society. On the first of the three morning sessions, Mrs. Harrison presided; on the other two, Mrs. William D. Cabell, Vice President General Presiding, took the chair. The Committee on Credentials reported the names of the 22 National Officers and 44 State and Chapter Regents and Delegates "present in the city . . . and . . . entitled to seats in the Congress. . . . two Honorary Regents are reported to be present and entitled to participate in the deliberations of the Congress but are not entitled to vote."

Highlights of reports by some of the National Officers:

Vice President General Presiding—a house for the Society. "It should be the finest building ever owned by women."

Recording Secretary General—a total of 24 Board meetings.

Corresponding Secretary General—received and answered more than 1800 letters; distributed about 7000 application blanks.

Registrars General—1306 members.

Treasurer General—on hand, $650 as the foundation of a permanent fund for the Society's building, leaving a balance of $776.66 "sufficient, probably, to meet all the ordinary expenses for the ensuing year."

Historian General—first Lineage Book ready for publication.

Later, the Historian General, Mrs. Lockwood, in her account of this Congress wrote:

This first Continental Congress was in every way unique and bearing but slight resemblance to the present orderly and dignified body. . . . Many of the delegates wanted the floor at the same time. And to wait for recognition from the Chair was almost an affront. They simply ignored parliamentary usage because they knew nothing about such rules. They would step out in the aisle, like an excited member of the United States Congress, and advance to the front to attract attention; while the presiding officer, equally inexperienced, had to be prompted, constantly, by the man at her elbow, with *Robert's Rules*.

(At the Board of Management meeting the following month, the use of the Society's office was offered to a class starting the study of parliamentary law for the convenience of DAR members.)

That Continental Congress adopted a single resolution:

WHEREAS, the Flag of our Country is the emblem of our Nation, and deserves the homage of every true American citizen; and

WHEREAS, the only distinctive national song we have is the "Star Spangled Banner"; be it therefore

RESOLVED, That we, the First Continental Congress of the Daughters of the American Revolution, earnestly request all American citizens, native born and adopted, whenever that song is sung or played in their presence, to show their respect and love for our country by rising and standing until it is finished.

RESOLVED FURTHER, That we also respectfully and earnestly recommend that the song be sung at least once a week in all the public schools of the United States, so that all American children may learn the words of the song, and learn to honor the Stars and Stripes.

The Charter granted the National Society, Daughters of the American Revolution by the Congress of the United States, and signed by President Grover Cleveland in 1896, authorized the Regents of the Smithsonian Institution "to permit said National Society to deposit its collections, manusripts, books, pamphlets, and other material for history in the Smithsonian Institution." These "relics" were moved to Memorial Continental Hall in 1909.

The spinning wheel that was the inspiration for the Society's Insignia is in the center of the illustration.

(Nearly forty years passed before "The Star-Spangled Banner" was officially designated as the national anthem by the Congress of the United States. During the House hearings in 1929, a NSDAR representative spoke in support of the bill, saying that since 1911 a resolution to this effect "had been passed unanimously by every congress of the Daughters of the American Revolution" that she could remember.)

The evening of February 24th, Mrs. Harrison gave a reception and supper for the regents and delegates at the White House, when the new china service designed by the First Lady was used for the first time. In the center of this china is an American eagle supported on a cloud; within the border are 44 stars representing the States at that time; gilt leaves, tassels, and ears of corn decorate the dark blue border. With this memorable social event, the President General of the Daughters of the American Revolution closed the First Continental Congress.

The *Philadelphia Inquirer* of March 28, 1892, reported the First Continental Congress as ". . . closing with an evening reception and supper given by Mrs. Harrison, the President of the Society, at the Executive Mansion. . . . The Daughters, about one hundred and twenty-five, and about ten gentlemen, the President also . . . [attended the] supper served in the private dining room, the historic china of the Jackson, Lincoln and Grant administrations was used, and also for the first time the new plates designed by Mrs. Harrison. . . ."

The great result of this First Continental Congress was the enthusiasm it aroused. Papers on many historic events and persons were read and enjoyed, and members from North and South and East and West intermingled and exchanged greetings. The sense of a common heritage in the Flag, of a common concern in the welfare of the country for which their forefathers fought side by side, made this meeting a memorable event for the Daughters who attended that First Continental Congress. As they boarded the trains for home after the two-day sessions, they took with them not only the recollections of their exciting experience but the impetus to arouse in others the same feelings for their heritage and country.

As this book goes to press, the Society is preparing for its Ninety-Fifth Continental Congress. A study of the Committee Chairmen's Reports in the *Annual Proceedings* of each Continental Congress would result in a comprehensive knowledge of committee pursuits during the Society's existence. There have been nearly 100 committees engaged in activities to promote the historical, educational and patriotic objectives of the NSDAR at state and chapter levels. Some committees automatically ceased to exist when they had served the purpose for which they were created; the work of others was absorbed by new committees reflecting the changing times; still others were reactivated in observance of national and international commemorations under new names; but many have existed continuously as, and since, they were created. The current committees, summarized in the preceding section, represent only a fraction of the total number. A detailed overview of *all* the committees created between the years 1890 and 1986 would fill another book.

White House Collection

International Gifts or Commemorations

Ever since the Society was founded, the Daughters have furthered their objectives by presenting gifts and observing commemorations relating to the history of our country and our allies. These have taken many forms. An early gift was the portrait of a First Lady.

Caroline Scott Harrison (Mrs. Benjamin Harrison), the Society's first President General and the wife of the President of the United States, died on October 25, 1892. As the most fitting tribute to her memory, the Daughters "decided to place her portrait in the White House, a gift to the nation." In 1894, during the third Continental Congress, the portrait of Mrs. Harrison, painted by Daniel Huntington, was unveiled upon the platform of the Church of Our Father, where she had presided. "As it afterwards passed down the aisle on its way to the White House the great assembly [100 Daughters representing 4,710 members] rose in silent homage and farewell."

The inscription on the plaque now reads:

> Caroline Scott Harrison
> Wife of President Benjamin Harrison
> Daniel Huntington (1816-1906)
> 1894
> Gift of the Daughters of American Revolution, 1894

The Society's first preservation effort was the appropriation, in 1896, of $100 to save historic Jamestown Island from being washed away by the James River. With this help, the Society for the Preservation of Virginia Antiquities was able to build a protective wall to preserve the site of the first successful settlement on this continent.

However, this was not the first contribution made by the DAR. That had been aiding the National Mary Washington Memorial Association to complete the memorial to George Washington's mother, and had been authorized during the organizational meetings of the Society in 1890. With generous donations from Daughters, the monument was erected at Fredericksburg, Virginia.

Toward the close of the 1890's, the Spanish-American War broke out. The NSDAR immediately offered to do anything to help the United States government. In reply, the Society was asked to alleviate the shortage of male nurses by examining women nurses who applied for service and preparing a list certifying those qualified. Dr. Anita Newcomb McGee, a member and officer of the Society, undertook to direct this project. A hospital corps was organized and 4,600 nurses were examined. Of these, 1,700 were certified. This marked the beginning of women nurses in the service of the United States, an endeavor that became the nucleus of the Army Nurse Corps. At the end of the Spanish-American War, those nurses who were not eligible for Government pensions, because they had served too short a time, received DAR pensions for as long as they lived. The DAR commemorates this significant contribution in establishing the Army Nurse Corps by awarding the Dr. Anita Newcomb McGee Medal annually to "The Nurse of the Year" selected by a board of the Army Medical Service.

The Federal government valued the wartime contributions made by the Society and called on the Daughters for peacetime patriotic endeavors as well.

As early as 1910, DAR members pioneered in assisting immigrants who lived in their local communities to become naturalized citizens. Many of these newcomers to America did not speak English and did not know how to become citizens. In order to help them, the NSDAR has compiled and published a *Manual for Citizenship* since 1921. A

DAR Steam Launch presented to the hospital ship, "Missouri," in the Spanish-American War.

DAR award known as the Americanism Medal is given to an outstanding naturalized adult who has been a citizen for at least five years.

In 1923, the DAR realized the need for keeping the immigrants busy at Ellis Island in New York Harbor, near the Statue of Liberty, and Angel Island on the Pacific Coast, while they waited, sometimes months, until medical and immigration authorities cleared them for admission into this country. The United States government granted the DAR permission to provide free material to those in the women's detention room at Ellis Island, and from this they made clothing for themselves and their children. The Daughters were given a connecting room for supplies. Daily, DAR volunteers passed lengths of cloth and balls of yarn through "the window of hope" to the waiting women. Soon the Daughters were asked to extend their work to include the men, who were particularly skilled at weaving scarves on the hand-made looms: a piece of wood studded with nails.

The United States Public Health Service asked the DAR to introduce this activity to the men in the U.S. Marine Hospital on Ellis Island. After Ellis Island and Angel Island were closed as immigration centers, the DAR continued occupational therapy work for twenty-eight years at the Marine Hospital on Ellis Island. The occupational therapy work that is carried on in government hospitals today is the result of this activity that was initiated by the DAR.

A DAR volunteer with a class in occupational therapy at the U.S. Marine Hospital, Ellis Island.

Another peacetime activity suggested by the Federal government was planting large areas with pine seedlings. Launched by the Daughters in 1938, small pines costing four dollars per thousand were planted to cover one acre of land. This project created 4,000 acres of Federal forest land. Tree planting has been a continuing activity of the Society. More recently, in 1984 a gift of 300 dogwood trees was presented to France. And, in 1985 an avenue of 50 elms were planted on the estate of the Duke of Buccleuch in Northampton, England. The site of the tree plantings had been used as a U.S. Army Air Field in World War II.

View of Memorial Continental Hall, Washington, taken by a United States naval aviator from an aeroplane in 1919. The Hall is in the left foreground; the American Red Cross building in the center, and the Corcoran Gallery of Art on the right. In the background, on the left, appears a section of the huge Munition Building, War Department. Directly behind Memorial Continental Hall is the temporary office building erected on DAR land for the use of the Council of National Defence.

The Spanish-American War, the first conflict in which the Daughters participated, has been followed by others with almost generational frequency.

During World War I, the Federal government erected a temporary war office building on National Headquarters land, which the DAR loaned to the United States. The Society gave $150,000 to Belgian Relief. DAR members and Chapters sponsored thousands of French war orphans: $200,000 was given for this purpose. (The names of these children are on file at DAR Headquarters.)

During World War II, the use of the DAR buildings was given to the American Red Cross. The furniture was moved out of the Period Rooms in Memorial Continental Hall and stored for the duration of the war. Constitution Hall was also used by the Red Cross. And a children's day nursery was set up in the basement of that building for enlisted men's wives who had to go to work.

The NSDAR is a member of the Veterans Administration Voluntary Service National Advisory Committee. DAR members serve as volunteers in Veterans Administration hospitals.

Patriotism is basic toward achieving the Society's goals. It is considered a patriotic, as well as educational, duty to assist newcomers to the United States to become citizens. The Society established an Americanization School in Washington, D.C. for this purpose. The earliest educational activity dates from 1908 when Miss Martha Berry appealed to the Daughters in behalf of her mountain children's school near Rome, Georgia. The Society's interest in Berry and other schools in Appalachia continues to this day.

Gifts to the United States and its allies, participation in commemorations at home and abroad, help to promote patriotism. From time to time since the beginning of this century, the DAR presents a Flag of the United States to the Senate or the House of Representatives in the Capitol, Washington, D.C., replacing them when necessary. Television viewers are familiar with this Flag, on the wall of the Speaker's rostrum in the House.

The Society was barely five years old when it was accorded an international patriotic honor. On July 4, 1900, the President General of the NSDAR officially represented the United States in Paris, France, by appointment of the President:

William McKinley, President of the United States of America, to all who shall see these presents, greeting. Know ye that, reposing special trust and confidence in the integrity and ability of Mrs. Daniel Manning, of New York, I do appoint her commissioner to represent the United States and the National Society of the Daughters of the American Revolution at the unveiling of the statue of Lafayette, and the presentation of a tablet for said statue at Paris, France, 1900, and at the Exposition there to be held, and do authorize and empower her to execute and fulfill the duties of that office according to law, and to have and to hold the said office with all the powers and privileges thereunto of rights appertaining unto her the said Mrs. Daniel Manning.

Under the joint resolution of Congress, approved February 23, 1900. In testimony whereof, I have caused these letters to be made patent and the seal of the United States to be hereunto affixed. Given under my hand at the City of Washington, the 23d day of February, in the year of our Lord one thousand nine hundred and of the Independence of the United States of America the one hundred and twenty-fourth.

By the President,

William McKinley.

John Hay,
    Secretary of State.

Medal commemorating the unveiling of the Statue of the Marquis de Lafayette in 1900. A replica of this medal was struck in 1983, the Bicentennial of the Treaty of Paris which established the independence of the United States.

The NSDAR has participated in more than a score of national and international expositions since 1893 when Daughters attended the World's Columbian Exposition in Chicago. In 1900, the Society's exhibit at the Paris Exposition won the Grand Prix. Most recently, the Society was represented at the Louisiana World Exposition in New Orleans in 1984.

The Society's emphasis on the American Revolution and, in particular, on that war's great military leader, George Washington, is illustrated by many gifts. The NSDAR furnished George Washington's house in Philadelphia during the Sesquicentennial Exposition in 1926; the Daughters presented an oil painting of Martha Washington to Lee Mansion in Arlington National Cemetery during George Washington's Bicentennial in 1932; and the DAR furnished the Surrender Room in the Moore House, Yorktown, Virginia, where the formal papers were signed on October 19, 1781, ending the American Revolutionary War.

Between 1928 and 1929, the DAR placed Madonna of the Trail monuments, 18 feet high, in each of twelve states across the country, from Maryland to California. The statue, by the sculptor Auguste Leimbach, is of a woman dressed in homespun holding her baby with her son by her side. They are located along the old trails used by the early settlers on their trek westward: Bethesda, Md.; Washington County, Pa.; Wheeling, W. Va.; Springfield, Ohio; Richmond, Ind.; Vandalia, Ill.; Lexington, Mo.; Council Grove, Kansas; Lamar, Colo.; Albuquerque, N. Mex.; Springerville, Arizona; and Upland, Calif.

Beginning in the late 1920s, when the Daughters saved the historic battlefield from a housing developer's bulldozers, Yorktown has been given special attention by the Society. At the Victory Monument in the National Military Park, the Society has, through the years, placed five tablets: one listing the names of the Americans, and another listing the names of the Frenchmen, who made the supreme sacrifice on the Yorktown battlefield; one to honor the men of the French fleet who died in the Yorktown campaign in the Battle Off the Virginia Capes; another to the Peacemakers, or Framers of the Treaty of Paris; and, lastly, one to the friends of the new nation as expressed by Benjamin Franklin, "We are now friends with England and all mankind."

The President General, Mrs. Russell William Magna, watches DAR banner being raised on the S.S. "Champlain," French liner, on which the DAR delegation sailed to pay tribute in Paris by placing a tablet in the French capital on October 19, 1932, to the French heroes who died in the Battle of Yorktown.

A major national project of the mid-1940s was building the Valley Forge Memorial Tower at Valley Forge, Pa., at the cost of more than half a million dollars, to honor American heroes, living and dead, of all wars. It is built of limestone and granite, stands 114 feet high, 24 feet square at the base, and consists of the Memorial Room, the Carillonneur's Room, and the Belfry.

In 1968, Mrs. William Henry Sullivan, Jr., President General, flew to the combat area of South Vietnam to represent the Daughters and emphasize their concern for our fighting men. There she awarded 47 DAR Medals to members of the United States Armed Forces.

In connection with commemorating the Bicentennial of the United States in 1976, the Society undertook several projects. The Rose Garden at Independence National Historical Park was dedicated to the Signers of the Declaration of Independence. Nearly 100 DAR members and guests accompanied the President General, Mrs. Erwin Frees Seimes, to attend the ceremonies in Philadelphia in 1971.

In 1972, during the Administration of Mrs. Donald Spicer, the Governor's Council Chamber and the Assembly Committee Room on the second floor of Independence Hall were furnished by the NSDAR as A Gift to the Nation project.

The Assembly Committee Room in Independence Hall, Philadelphia

This was followed by A Bicentennial Tribute to the United States of America which is a permanent work of art in the United States Capitol. Begun in the Administration of Mrs. Henry Stewart Jones (1974-1975), it was completed in the Administration of Mrs. Wakelee Rawson Smith (1975-1977).

The murals, by Allyn Cox, are in the ceiling of the East-West Corridor of the House Wing of the Capitol, which extends a distance of some 200 feet. Chronicled in the 16 murals that measure 6 feet by 8 feet are scenes depicting legislative milestones of 300 years, from the Signing of the Mayflower Compact in 1620 to the Enactment of Woman Suffrage in 1920, both of which are pictured here.

The others are: Albany Congress, First Continental Congress, Declaration of Independence, Constitutional Convention, First Federal Congress, George Washington Inauguration, George Washington Farewell Address, Monroe Doctrine, Second Lincoln Inaugural, Smithsonian Institution, Old Library of Congress, Iron Foundry, and Amphibious Digger.

Courtesy The Office of the Architect, U.S. Capitol

In addition to the 16 murals there are 32 vignettes, on either side of each mural, complimenting the historic scenes. In the ceiling 16 medallion portraits are painted in appropriate chronology, and succinct quotations appear above the 16 corridor doorways.

Important dates and events in the history of our Nation and of our allies and friends have been the impetus for a variety of NSDAR activities. Tilloloy, a small village in France, had been destroyed during World War I and the Society had pledged itself to rebuild the water supply. In addition, 60 houses were completely furnished and livestock was supplied to the villagers. In 1921, Mrs. George Maynard Minor, then President General, dedicated the project which had cost $50,000. Sixty-one years later, Mrs. Richard Denny Shelby, President General, visited Tilloloy and laid a wreath at the War Memorial in the village cemetery.

A Peacemaker Award was established in 1983, in observance of the Bicentennial of the Treaty of Paris, to be presented to an individual who exemplified the principles of freedom, peace, understanding, and love of fellowman.

In August-September 1983, more than 200 Daughters traveled to Paris to celebrate the Bicentennial of the Treaty of Paris and dedicated a marker at Yorktown Square honoring Peacemakers Benjamin Franklin, John Jay, and John Adams. In addition to formal ceremonies which included a visit to the Marquis de Lafayette's grave, a reception at the City Hall, and the placing of wreaths at several sites, the National Society hosted a midnight dinner in the Hall of Battles at Versailles which was attended by more than 500 guests, many of whom were French, and representatives from all the nations who had participated in the Treaty of Paris.

The President General, Mrs. Walter Hughey King, is shown at the reception in City Hall, following her address, made at the request of M. Jacques Chirac, Mayor of Paris, with (left) Mme. Guy de Montlaur; State Regent of France; Mrs. Douglas MacArthur (center); Mrs. Charles Robb; Senator John Warner, Personal Representative of the President of the United States to the Treaty of Paris Bicentennial Celebration; the Honorable Charles Robb, Governor of Virginia.

Members of the National Society, Daughters of the American Revolution marched down the Champs Élysées to the Tomb of France's Unknown Soldier at the Arc de Triomphe led by the President General, Mrs. Walter Hughey King.

There were several commemorative events in 1985 that took place outside the United States. In June, a group of Daughters travelled to England to represent the Society in the presentation of a plaque at St. Peter's Church in Wolverhampton to recognize the church where Button Gwinnett, a Signer of the Declaration of Independence, married and where his three daughters were baptised. In August, the Society dedicated a bronze marker in memory of the American soldiers who died at Trois-Rivières, Canada, on June 8, 1776. The marker is in the park facing the Place de l'Hotel de Ville. The members of the Ursuline Order were presented a plaque in gratitude for the care given by its nuns to the American soldiers wounded at the Battle of Trois-Rivières. In December, the Society presented a showcase table for the open register in All Hallows Church, London, England for displaying the marriage license of Louisa Catherine Johnson and John Quincy Adams.

On her official visit to Hawaii in February, 1986, the President General presented a bronze plaque to be placed on the "SS Arizona." And in April, 1986, the plaque commemorating the designation of Constitution Hall as a National Historic Landmark will be dedicated.

More than half a million dollars has been donated by the Daughters as a gift from the Society to the restoration of the Statue of Liberty. The project is to be completed in 1986, the 100th birthday of the internationally famous statue. Photo by Larry Bellante